PRC

MW01533848

YOUR

ASSETS

PROTECT YOUR
ASSETS

How to Avoid Falling Victim to the Government's Forfeiture Laws

Adam Starchild

Paladin Press · Boulder, Colorado

Also by Adam Starchild:

Keep What You Own: Protect Your Money, Property, and Family
   from Courts, Creditors, and the IRS
Reviving the American Dream:
   Stop "Just Getting By" and Build Real Wealth
Swiss Money Secrets:
   How You Can Legally Hide Your Money in Switzerland
Using Offshore Havens for Privacy and Profits

Protect Your Assets:
   How to Avoid Falling Victim to the Government's Forfeiture Laws
by Adam Starchild

Copyright © 1996 by Adam Starchild

ISBN 0-87364-906-0
Printed in the United States of America

Published by Paladin Press, a division of
Paladin Enterprises, Inc., P.O. Box 1307,
Boulder, Colorado 80306, USA.
(303) 443-7250

Direct inquiries and/or orders to the above address.

PALADIN, PALADIN PRESS, and the "horse head" design
are trademarks belonging to Paladin Enterprises and
registered in United States Patent and Trademark Office.

CONTENTS

Civil Asset Forfeiture

Any property-owning U.S. citizen, and any investor with property located in the United States, must become knowledgeable about the threat of civil asset forfeiture—government's police power to confiscate your real and personal property based on that property's alleged use or involvement in criminal activities.

The threat of government confiscation applies to homeowners; landlords; people with resort condos; investors or partners in hotels, restaurants, and bars; and those who own farm or undeveloped land. Even retail business and commercial property owners are at serious risk.

For people concerned about protecting their wealth, particularly real estate, avoidance of potential asset forfeiture is a compelling reason to take careful preventive action—or to avoid certain types of real estate investments completely. As you will see, avoidance of civil asset forfeiture is not an easy task, especially because of investor complacency based on a traditional belief in a host of U.S. constitutional safeguards protecting private property ownership. Alarmingly, many of these former legal protections have collapsed under the pressure of a growing American police state.

CONSTITUTIONAL SAFEGUARDS?

The practical American colonial experience with the despotism of the British Crown and its agents produced the Fifth Amendment to the United States Constitution, part of our nation's Bill of Rights, which declares the following:

> No person shall be deprived of life, liberty or
> property without due process of law; nor shall
> property be taken for public use, without just
> compensation.

Today this historic guarantee is mocked by events unknown to much of the general public but very real to those suffering in the grip of federal, state, and local law enforcement agencies engaged in the systematic degradation of the constitutional guarantees of property rights.

Civil asset forfeiture laws are being enforced with Gestapo-like zeal by state and federal police authorities and courts in a highly unjust manner. These questionable official acts, literally robbing private citizens, depend for their dubious authority on a combination of musty legal doctrines dating back to early English common law and the eagerness of contemporary politicians to "get tough" on crime and drugs, even at the expense of personal liberty.

These widespread injustices multiply daily all over America. Enlisted 20 years ago as an auxiliary tool in the so-called "war on drugs," the legal doctrines of civil asset forfeiture have been perverted to an entirely improper function in our democratic system of government. In the United States today, forfeiture literally means wholesale government confiscation of private property—especially real property—by law enforcement agencies, usually without any formal charge of criminal conduct having been filed against the affected property owner and with little or no recourse available to the affected property owner.

WHAT IS FORFEITURE?

A standard legal dictionary definition of "forfeiture" (until a few years ago) would have been the "loss of some right or property as a penalty for some illegal act." Whether you call it forfeiture, confiscation, expropriation, or commandeering, it all amounts to the same thing: government now has the arbitrary power to seize almost any privately owned property. Property is in danger of seizure if it was 1) allegedly purchased with the proceeds of illegal activity, 2) allegedly used to "facilitate" criminal activity, or 3) alleged to be the location of criminal activity.

The word "alleged" is emphasized because the statutory and judicial procedures governing forfeitures allow police to seize your property *prior* to any hearing before a judge or magistrate and to keep the property without charging you with any crime. They have the right to retain it until *you* are able to prove your property is not tainted by criminal conduct.

Much of what you may have learned in the past about your guaranteed rights and liberties no longer applies to property rights. Increased government and police powers, the perception of rising criminal activity and violence, popular anxiety about drug use—all these have become the political justifications for curtailing the application of the Bill of Rights and the individual security it once guaranteed. Police and government agents now have the power to seize your business, home, bank account, records, and personal property, all without prior indictment, hearing, or trial. Everything you possess can be taken away at the whim of one or two state or federal officials who may target you secretly. Regardless of sex, age, race, or economic status, we are all just a knock on the door away from becoming potential victims of civil asset forfeiture and its abuse.

In Part One of this book, you'll learn the details and history of these forfeitures. In Part Two you'll find a number of specific techniques that you can apply to protect your property from forfeiture.

CHAPTER

1

Not Just the War on Drugs

For 20 years the American news media have gleefully reported the confiscation of hundreds of millions of dollars of "laundered" drug money, bank accounts, expensive yachts, jet planes, waterfront homes, and fancy cars allegedly belonging to "drug lords." Real-life scenes of police raids right out of "Miami Vice" caught the popular imagination, and now television is overloaded with shows glorifying cops breaking down doors and shouting "POLICE!" or "FBI!" The underlying theme is always the fight to conquer drugs.

Lest you believe the mistaken notion that asset forfeiture only concerns drug-related crimes, you should know there are now more than 100 different federal forfeiture statutes addressing a wide range of illegal conduct, both criminal and civil. These laws range from the forfeiture of animals seized from animal fighting impresarios ("cock fighting") and untaxed contraband cigarettes seized from interstate smugglers to the seizure of firearms for gun law infractions and the taking of property acquired from violations of the Racketeer Influenced and Corrupt Organizations Act (better known as RICO).

Some of the federal government agencies with statutory forfeiture power include the Drug Enforcement Administration (DEA) and the U.S. Customs Bureau of the Treasury Department, the Federal Bureau of Investigation (FBI), U.S. Coast Guard, the U.S. Postal Service (USPS), the Bureau of Land Management (BLM) and the Fish and Wildlife Bureau [both in the Department of Interior (DOI)], the Securities and Exchange Commission (SEC), the Department of Health and Human Services (HHS), the Food and Drug Administration (FDA), the Justice Department (including the Immigration and Naturalization Service), the Department of Housing and Urban Development (HUD), and, of course, the Internal Revenue Service (IRS), plus more than 3,000 state and local police departments.

WATCH OUT FOR NEW JERSEY

New Jersey is a state with one of the most severe forfeiture laws, triggered by *any* alleged criminal conduct, even shoplifting. That statute denies the right to a trial by jury on the issue of forfeiture. Its application is so severe that a male gynecologist, Owen A. Chang, M.D., accused of conducting a medical exam of a female patient without the presence of a nurse, as required by local law, had his office equipment and building confiscated. Kathy Schrama, accused of stealing UPS packages worth at most $500 from her neighbors' doorsteps in New Jersey, saw local police take away her home, two cars, and all her furniture—even the Christmas presents she had purchased for her 10-year-old son. A building contractor who bid on, received, properly executed, and was paid for several construction contracts for New Jersey municipalities, later had his entire business confiscated by the state based on an allegation that his company was not legally qualified to make the bids in the first place.

Arizona's statutes are also an example of the trend in abandoning any distinction between civil and criminal forfeiture, applying unlimited forfeiture with few procedural protections for property owners as a handy supplement to criminal law enforcement. The state's assistant attorney general, Cameron Holmes, proudly describes his state's law as "a stride in the evolution of a 'civil justice system' to complement the 'criminal justice system' through judicial intervention in antisocial behavior." This is the sort of exceedingly fuzzy thinking that has served to expand property confiscation and shrink personal legal protection and freedom.

EXPANSION OF FORFEITURE CRIMES

Not content with applying forfeiture law to drug offenses, legislators and prosecutors are rapidly expanding the forfeiture principle to cover a host of alleged criminal acts in every area of activity. A growing number of states, including Texas, New Jersey, and Florida, now apply civil forfeiture to *any* criminal activity, which means owners must police their real property against all criminal activity—or possibly lose it. Homeowners and landlords are not only being forced into the role of "their brother's keeper" but held responsible for the acts of their children, spouses, guests, and tenants—and even their tenant's guests.

Make a mistake on a loan application and you may face forfeiture. In an attempt to curb savings and loan fraud, in 1989 Congress made it a criminal offense to give false information on a loan application. Now this law is being used by the government to confiscate the property financed with loan proceeds, even years later, and even if all payments are up to date. Under this loan application law, in Florida in 1991, the U.S. Marshal's Service seized $11 million worth of commercial property, including five convenience stores, a multiplex movie theater, and a consumer electronics store.

Asset forfeiture is now being applied to the real and personal property of doctors and other health care professionals suspected of fraud related to Medicare and Medicaid programs, allowing even the seizure of patients' private medical records. Similar criminal forfeiture provisions were included in President Clinton's proposed 1994 National Health Security Act, allowing jail sentences, fines, and forfeiture of any property facilitating newly created health care "crimes."

To give you an idea of how far this has gone, in 1993 a federal circuit court ruled that defendants charged with illegally modifying, selling, and using television signal "descramblers" (which allow satellite dishes to pick up coded TV signals) were violating federal wiretapping laws. Such acts are not only felonies but forfeitable crimes, meaning your house could be taken away if you install a TV signal descrambler.

As you are beginning to see, the possibilities of you and your property being ensnared by government forfeiture are endless.

The Official Government Line

Aside from the standard argument about the imperative need to fight the unending and unsuccessful war on drugs, the sole defense offered by federal and state officials supporting asset forfeiture laws is that the complaints of unjust treatment are only isolated "aberrations," certainly not typical of the way in which these laws are generally administered.

This was the view of George Terwilliger III, associate attorney general in charge of the U.S. Department of Justice's asset forfeiture program during the Bush administration. Terwilliger admitted only that in some few cases "dumb judgment" might have created problems for individual property owners. "That's why we have the courts," he said. A similar defensive line was followed by Cary Copeland, director of the Justice Department's Office of Asset Forfeiture, who blames forfeiture opposition on criminal defense attorneys who "aren't interested in justice but are interested in dismantling the program that takes money out of their pockets."

But in their unguarded moments, even the federal officials responsible for administration of the forfeiture laws admit what's really going on. Copeland told *Newsweek* magazine that as a revenue raiser the forfeiture program "is the goose that lays the golden egg." Former Bush-administration Director of the Asset Forfeiture Office Michael F. Zeldin told a 1993 conference on white collar crime, "We had a situation in which the desire to deposit money into the asset forfeiture fund became the raison d'etre of forfeiture, eclipsing in certain measure the desire to effect fair enforcement of the laws."

THE AVERAGE AMERICAN PAYS

Most cavalier official statements try to make you believe that average Americans are not suffering because of asset forfeiture, that only sinister "drug kingpins" are the victims of the law. The truth is that the vast majority of forfeitures involve property belonging to innocent average citizens caught in the clutches of this draconian law and its eager enforcers.

Consider the figures released by the U.S. Drug Enforcement Agency for the 18 months ending in December 1990, which showed that only 17 percent of the 25,297 items seized by DEA were valued in excess of $50,000. Further evidence that the majority of the people who suffer from civil asset forfeiture are average Americans, not rich criminals nor even drug lords, came in documents obtained under the state Freedom of Information Act by officials of the Michigan Association for the Preservation of Property (MAPP). In 1992 Michigan law enforcement agencies used civil forfeiture in 9,770 instances and confiscated an average of only $1,434 per seizure. They seized a total of $14,007,227 in cash and property, up from the 1991 total of $11,848,547. Property taken included 54 private homes (up from 29 homes in 1991) with an average value of $15,881 (this in a nation where the national average price for a home is now more than $100,000). Autos seized totaled 807, with an average value of $1,412—not exactly luxury models. A total of 8,909 seizures produced $9,225,515 in cash and other negotiable instruments and only $2,754,818 in personal property. An examination of records showed that seizures were not contested, mainly because the value of the cash and property confiscated in most cases was too low to justify the $5,000 to $10,000 in attorney fees and court costs such a challenge would require. Of the 123 separate police agencies reporting, only one, the Muskegon Police Narcotics Department, gave any detailed accounting of the number of arrests made. No police department gave any evidence of convictions obtained associated with the forfeitures. The Muskegon Police seized cash 72 times for a total of $31,199 and an average for each seizure of $433. Tom Flook, an official of MAPP, commented, "Obviously, most civil forfeitures in Michigan are not much more than curbside shakedowns."

In 1992 the Committee on Public Safety of the California State Assembly made the following statement in a majority report on legislation aimed at curbing that state's asset forfeiture program: "Asset forfeiture is a multimillion dollar source of revenue for [California] law enforcement. Thus, there is an incentive to seize property as a revenue source . . . persons suspected of participation in, or having knowledge of drug crimes rarely will be given the benefit of the doubt by those who will gain financially by the seizure. This is viewed as a particular problem in times of tight budgets." Republican Assemblyman Charles Quackenbush said, "To take property from people who haven't been convicted of anything is an outrageous abuse of police power." His colleague, Assemblyman David Knowles, one the most conservative Republicans in the legislature, agreed: "This isn't about law and order. This is an issue of property rights. This is about police kicking down peoples' doors and taking their money. It's tyrannical government run amok."

One federal judge recently assessed the problem correctly when he noted that the vast quantity and value of the assets that have been seized by police overall under forfeiture laws rightfully "leads some observers to question whether we are seeing fair and effective law enforcement or an insatiable appetite for a source of increased revenue." There is little doubt it's the revenue the police are after.

IT ALL ADDS UP—WAY UP

As you consider how to protect your own assets, keep in mind that we are not talking about small numbers here. Lest you think the value of all this confiscated property is negligible, consider this: between 1986 and 1990, the U.S. Department of Justice took in $1.5 billion from forfeitures. (That's *billion* with a "b"). In 1992 the total was $531 million. During fiscal year 1992 the U.S. Customs Bureau seized property valued in excess of $708 million. These figures do not include the billions of dollars of property taken by state and local government agencies. As the *Pittsburgh Press* so aptly put it, "The billions of dollars that forfeiture brings into law enforcement agencies is so blinding that it obscures the devastation it causes the innocent."

The amount deposited in the U.S. Department of Justice Asset Forfeiture Fund increased from $27 million in fiscal year 1985 to $531 million in 1992. Of the amount taken in 1992, $362 million was in cash and $114 million was proceeds from the disposal of forfeited property. $230 million of the total was returned to state and local law enforcement agencies that assisted in investigations leading to forfeitures. And $30 million in forfeited property (planes, boats, cars, and so on) was pressed into official use by federal law enforcement agencies or transferred to state and local police for their use.

Real Estate: A Major Target

In 1993 the U.S. Department of Justice had on hand an inventory in excess of 32,400 separate real properties, ranging from luxury waterfront homes in Florida to crack houses in Philadelphia, with a combined value of more than $1.8 billion. The U.S. Customs Service seized more than $708 million worth of property in fiscal year 1992, including, among others, the entire Indian Wells Country Club, Resort Hotel, and 27-hole golf course in the southern California desert, and the 18-hole Royal Kenfield Golf Course in Las Vegas, Nevada. In July 1994 in Florida, the Tampa city government publicly celebrated with great fanfare the confiscation of the 100th private building or residence alleged to be a crack house or drug den. (Notice was sent to the owners of record, and failure to respond resulted in the city's confiscating the house and tearing it down.)

Under asset forfeiture, hotels have been taken because one room was used for a drug transaction. Apartment houses have been confiscated because drug deals allegedly took place in some unspecified apartments. Three houses owned and run by Greek fraternities at the University of Virginia were seized by local police based on alleged sales of small quantities of drugs by student frat members. At one point, under a now dead federal drug enforcement policy known as "zero tolerance," which was instituted during the Reagan administration, the oceanographic research vessel *Atlantis* was seized by the Coast Guard off the coast of Massachusetts because of the discovery of a single marijuana cigarette in the ship's crew quarters.

Similarly, in California, a Scripps Oceanographic Institute research vessel was seized because a marijuana "roach" was found in the locker of a sailor who had long before been fired.

On June 8, 1994, federal authorities seized a run-down, 22-story, 621-room hotel near Gramercy Park in New York City based on alleged drug trafficking and "violence." The building, valued at more than $2.5 million, had been the scene of more than 122 police arrests since 1991, but the U.S. Attorney's office, bragging that this "represented the largest [property] seizure in the nation," admitted police had been unable to stem drug activity—therefore they confiscated the building. Query: if the police cannot control crime at a particular location over a period of three years with 122 arrests, how can the building owner be expected to do what the police cannot? And why should police failure be rewarded by confiscation of this multimillion dollar property for government benefit?

Under such outrageous applications of the law, nothing is safe from government seizure—not homes, boats, airplanes, gambling casinos, banks, businesses, or dormitories at Harvard or Yale.

CHAPTER

2

Police Conflict of Interest

Prior to the adoption of the Comprehensive Crime Control Act of 1984, the money realized from civil asset forfeiture was deposited in the general fund of the U.S. Treasury. Now it primarily goes to the Department of Justice's Asset Forfeiture Fund (with some paid into the Department of the Treasury's Forfeiture Fund). The money is then supposed to be used for forfeiture-related expenses and general law enforcement purposes, with no further congressional appropriations or authorization being necessary.

This is where a grievous problem arose—the police were allowed to keep all the proceeds from the property they confiscated, an open and excessive invitation to uncontrollable abuse. Now, the same police authorities who confiscate the property spend most of these billions as they please, with little or no outside supervision or control, but with plenty of incentive to push more and profitable forfeitures to the maximum. It goes without saying—allowing law enforcement agencies to keep any cash or property they can confiscate creates a built-in conflict of interest of the greatest magnitude.

Giving police this enormous power allowed them to begin the war against the private property of innocent Americans, not just the "proceeds of crime" or the assets of convicted criminals. The popularity of asset forfeiture among police—armed with statutory authorization and with no legislative oversight over how the money is spent—immediately skyrocketed. This not only gave the police the power to terrorize innocent citizens, it also allowed them to finance their own new police state out of the property they seized.

AN AMERICAN POLICE STATE

You may be shaking your head in disbelief at this point, asking yourself whether you should believe such things could happen in America. Believe it. There are thousands of examples of government forfeiture actions that have had terrible consequences, including death, involving many thousands of innocent Americans. The following is a representative sampling:

•   Willie Jones, the owner of a landscaping service, is African-American. On February 27, 1991, he paid for his airplane ticket in cash at the Nashville Metro Airport. This "suspicious" behavior—a black man paying cash— caused the ticket agent to alert Nashville police. (Ticket agents are paid police rewards for turning in "suspicious" people.) A police search of Jones and his luggage yielded no drugs. However, he did have $9,600 in cash in his wallet, on which a sniffing police dog detected traces of drugs (a chemical condition true of 80 to 90 percent of all U.S. currency now in circulation). His cash was promptly seized, despite protestations by Jones that, as was his business custom, he intended to use the money to purchase plants and shrubbery from growers in Houston, Texas, the destination for which he had purchased his round-trip plane ticket, an annual event. No arrest was made. However, the seizure nearly drove Jones out of business. He was unable to post the 10 percent bond money ($960) necessary to mount a legal challenge, and the DEA refused to return his cash. He sued the DEA for discrimination based on his race, and in April 1993, more than two years later, a federal judge ordered his $9,600 returned, noting that the presence of drugs on currency is so prevalent as to be meaningless as a justification for forfeiting cash.

• On April 9, 1989, Jacksonville, Florida, university professor Craig Klein's new $24,000 sailboat was "inspected" in what turned out to be a fruitless drug search by U.S. Customs Service agents. In their seven-hour rampage, they damaged the boat beyond repair. Using axes, power drills, and crowbars, they dismantled the engine, ruptured the fuel tank, and drilled more than 30 holes in the hull— half of them below the water line. Not only did the Customs Service refuse to compensate the Kleins, one of the agents later phoned the professor and threatened his life if he complained to his congressman about these events. Mr. Klein was forced to sell the ship for scrap. Through the efforts of U.S. Rep. Charles Bennett of Florida, Congress passed a private claim bill granting Klein $8,900—small recompense for his economic loss and the efforts he was forced to make to defend his liberty.

• For many years Billy and Karon Munnerlyn owned and operated an air charter service out of Las Vegas, Nevada. In October 1989, Mr. Munnerlyn was hired to fly Albert Wright from Little Rock, Arkansas, to Ontario, California. DEA agents seized Wright's luggage and found $2.7 million inside. Both he and Mr. Munnerlyn were arrested, and all of Munnerlyn's office records were confiscated by the DEA, as was his $8,500 charter fee for the flight. Though the charges against Munnerlyn were quickly dropped for lack of evidence, the government refused to release the airplane. (The charges against Wright, who was, unbeknownst to Munnerlyn, a convicted cocaine dealer, were eventually dropped as well.) Munnerlyn spent more than $85,000 in legal fees trying to get his plane back—money he raised by selling his three other planes. Though a Los Angeles jury awarded him the return of his airplane because they found he had no knowledge that he was transporting drug money, a U.S. district judge reversed the jury's verdict. Munnerlyn was forced to declare bankruptcy and is now driving a truck for a living. He eventually spent $7,000 to buy his plane back. However, the DEA caused about $100,000 of damage to the plane. The agency is not liable for the damage, and Mr. Munnerlyn has been unable to raise the money to restart his business.

- Official findings of the Ventura County, California, district attorney's office concluded that multimillionaire Donald Scott of Malibu was shot to death by state and federal agents during a mistaken drug raid at his home, brought about in part because the U.S. National Park Service wanted to confiscate his 200-acre ranch adjacent to the Santa Monica Mountains National Recreation Area—land which he had repeatedly refused to sell to the government.

   A little before 9:00 A.M. on the morning of October 2, 1992, the 61-year-old Scott was shot dead in front of his wife when 30 local, state, and federal agents burst into his home and attempted to serve him with a search warrant enabling them to inspect his ranch for suspected cultivation of marijuana. Scott, who was upstairs dressing, responded to his wife's screams for help, and brandished a handgun as he came downstairs during the confusion of the raid.

   After a five-month investigation, Ventura County District Attorney Michael Bradbury concluded that the police, including the Los Angeles County Sheriff's deputy who shot Scott to death, never had any evidence of drug cultivation and had obtained the search warrant for the raid by illegally withholding that lack of evidence from the judge who signed the warrant. He also found that the police-provided affidavits given the judge in support of the warrant request were either false or misleading. Both actions constitute criminal conduct in California, although no one was subsequently charged with these crimes or the death of Mr. Scott.

Nicholas Gutue, the executor of Scott's estate, noting that Scott was known to be "fanatically anti-drug," pointed out that the deceased had repeatedly refused to sell his $5 million scenic ranch to the U.S. National Park Service, which wanted to add the land to the adjacent Santa Monica Mountains National Recreation Area. U.S. Park Service officers took part in the combined county, state, and federal police raid, even though they had no legal jurisdiction to do so. Bradbury concluded that at the final police briefing just before the raid, the possible government seizure of Scott's ranch was discussed by two police agents and a U.S. forest ranger and that documents they reviewed included a property appraisal statement and a parcel map showing adjacent land sales in the area. This preraid interest in confiscation of the Scott ranch was also born out in documents uncovered by reporters for CBS television's "60 Minutes," which aired a segment on the raid on April 2, 1993. The district attorney concluded: "We find no reason why the law enforcement officers who were investigating suspected narcotics violation have any interest in the value of the ranch or the value of property sold in the same area other than if they had a motive to forfeit the property."

It is more than frightening to realize that based on such a banal, bureaucratic motive, federal, state, and local police would not only violate laws they are sworn to uphold, but would kill an innocent man in the process. All of this because forfeiture law admits the

possibility of confiscating a citizen's home, which faceless bureaucrats and their police accomplices covet. What greater evidence of
the perversion of government power, of the advent of the police
state, could there be?

POLICE VIOLENCE

Such official corruption and criminal conduct might be easier to
understand were this an isolated example. But it is not. These events
are widespread in every part of the United States. Nor are those subjected to such illegal police activities usually people of wealth such as
the late Donald Scott. The sad truth is that the vast majority of citizens affected by such police misconduct are average people who happen to be in the wrong place at the wrong time—ironically, not
unlike the victims of crime generally in this unfortunate day and age.

For example, on the night of August 25, 1992, in Poway,
California, a U.S. Customs Service drug raid, complete with numerous heavily armed DEA agents, broke down the door of Donald L.
Carlson's suburban San Diego county home. Aroused from sleep and
thinking a robbery was underway, Carlson grabbed a gun as the
agents smashed the door and lobbed a percussion grenade into his
home. In an exchange of gunfire, Carlson was hit three times—in
the arm, lung, and femoral vein. After three weeks on a ventilator
in intensive care, he was lucky to be alive. He will suffer lifelong
diaphragm paralysis, chronic pain, and circulatory problems.

There were no drugs in Carlson's house, and for good reason:
he has no criminal record, has never used illegal drugs, is a vice president of a leading Fortune 500 company, and is a family man
respected by friends and associates. But Carlson had been fingered
falsely by a paid informer (known as "Ron") who had already been
kicked out of one federal anti-drug program because he filed two
other false reports—one fingering a vacant house! After the shoot-
ing, Carlson's neighbors heard one agent tell another, "Now get the
story straight: he shot first." Carlson has filed suit for damages and
alleges that there is a government conspiracy to cover up the
Customs Service blunder. No one has been charged with any wrongdoing as a result of this tragic event.

TROUBLE IN PARADISE

Innocent people of limited means often lose everything in forfeiture cases. In 1991, four years after the mentally unstable 28-year-old son of a Maui couple pleaded guilty and was placed on probation for growing marijuana in the backyard of his parents' home where he lived, a Maui police detective was combing through old police records looking for possible forfeiture cases. For the Maui police, like other law agencies, forfeiture means immediate control of assets and money for the department to spend pretty much as it pleases. Because 65-year-old retired Joseph Lopes and his 60-year-old wife, Francis, admitted they knew their son was growing pot (even though they tried to get him to stop), the Maui police saw legal grounds on which to take the couple's home. With the five-year statute of limitations still on their side, the police began a civil forfeiture claim in February, 1991. Lopes, a sugar plantation worker, had worked for 30 years living in rented company housing while saving to buy his own home. In 1987 when their son, Thomas, was arrested and placed on probation for the pot offense, forfeiture was rarely used by police anywhere. Now, as Assistant U.S. Attorney Marshall Silverberg of Honolulu readily admitted, the government sees an attractive financial payoff in forfeiture and uses it. Police and prosecutors regularly comb through old case records looking for forfeiture possibilities. With a remarkable touch of official arrogance, Silverberg told a reporter, "I concede the time lapse on this case is longer than most, but there was a violation, and that makes this appropriate, not money-grubbing." Then, with a supreme touch of charity (if not chutzpah), the government lawyer added, "The other way to look at this, you know, is the Lopeses should be happy we let them live there as long as we did." The couple's attorney, Matthew Menzer, says he has eight other cases in which the police have gone back years, resurrecting cases involving small-time crimes for forfeiture actions. "Digging these cases out now is a business proposition, not law enforcement," says Menzer.

People in business are also victims. Michael Sandsness and his wife, Christine, owned two gardening supply stores called Rain & Shine in Eugene and Portland, Oregon. Among the items sold were metal halide grow lights, used for growing many indoor plants. The grow lights also can be used to grow marijuana, but it is not illegal to sell them. Because some area marijuana gardens raided by DEA had the lights, the agency began building a case to seize the gardening supply business. In early 1991 the DEA sent undercover agents to the stores, who tried without success to get employees to give advice on growing marijuana. Finally, agents engaged an employee in conversation, asking advice on the amount of heat or noise generated by the lights, making oblique comments suggesting they wanted to avoid detection and commenting about *High Times* magazine. They never actually mentioned marijuana. The employee then sold the agents grow lights. DEA then raided the two stores, seizing inventory and bank accounts. Agents told the landlord of one of the stores that if he did not evict Sandsness, the government would seize his building, and the landlord reluctantly complied. While the forfeiture case was pending, the business was destroyed. Mr. Sandsness was forced to sell the remaining inventory not seized in order to pay off creditors.

In the summer of 1993, New York police began confiscating automobiles with loud radios that violated a city noise ordinance. You can bet the cars confiscated weren't those belonging to elderly deaf folks blasting Beethoven or Bach. More likely the targets were African-American and Latino teenagers booming rap with a heavy baseline beat—in itself, a discriminatory distinction that would violate the Equal Protection Clause of the Fourteenth Amendment.

On March 12, 1993, 37 separate U.S. Food and Drug Administration commando-style raids were conducted in 23 cities, replete with G-men in black flak jackets brandishing automatic weapons. The targets: the professional offices of licensed medical doctors who prescribe holistic, herbal, vitamin, and other "health supplement" therapies held suspect by FDA bureaucrats. Inventories and patient records were seized, and, in one case, the office staff was held for six hours at gunpoint while the search proceeded.

In Los Angeles in 1993, police raided the medical offices of more than 50 doctors, confiscating medical records and files, looking for workmen's compensation law violations.

UNFAIR COMPETITION

The potential for personal and commercial harm resulting from police abuse of forfeiture is demonstrated by what happened to Jim Spurlock, owner of an aircraft sales company in Fort Worth, Texas. In 1992 U.S. Customs officials seized airplanes valued at more than a half million dollars each that Spurlock had sold to two customers, based on an informant's tips alleging that a Brazilian drug smuggler was involved. One, a Learjet, sold in January and about to be flown to Brazil, supposedly contained a large hidden stash of cash. Customs agents seized the plane, found no money, but held the aircraft for seven months on the pretext that the plane's Federal Aviation Administration (FAA) registration documents had been falsely executed. (On one form the purchaser had checked the "corporation" box instead of the "foreign corporation" box, thus misrepresenting himself.) Before the government would return the plane, it demanded and got a $16,000 "impoundment fee" from the plane purchaser, who was also stuck with substantial legal fees and damage repairs exceeding $35,000. Another plane Spurlock sold was similarly seized by Customs on a FAA paper technicality and also had to be ransomed by its owner. The most disturbing aspect of this story of high-handed Customs conduct was revealed later when Spurlock discovered that the informant's tip came from one of his business competitors, who later openly bragged about using the government to disrupt Spurlock's business.

Local artist Judy Enright of Ann Arbor, Michigan, had one of her painting/collages seized from an art show by agents of the U.S. Fish and Wildlife Service because it was decorated with feathers from migratory birds. She had gathered the feathers, for which their former owners presumably had no further use, in her own backyard and nearby woods. The ever vigilant federal agents informed her possession of such feathers violates the 1918 Migratory Bird Treaty and its implementation law.

AUTOS: A SPECIALTY

Police confiscation of autos for forfeiture has become a lucrative (for the police) national trend. Autos are easy to seize and valuable for quick sale unless the car title is encumbered by loans (in which case the police will usually return the car rather than mess with the paperwork and bank payoff). The police know that when they confiscate a paid-for 1990 Honda Civic with a Blue Book value of $9,050, the owner—unless he or she is very angry or very wealthy, or both—is not going to spend $10,000 in legal fees, storage costs, and repairs to get the car back. In Houston, Texas, more than 4,000 cars are confiscated each year, and in New York City, more than 10,000 are. Special police auto confiscation units have been established in Texas, New York, New Jersey, Alabama, Arizona, California, and many other states.

A 1988 examination of these practices in just one Florida county, Pinellas, in the Tampa Bay area, by the *St. Petersburg Times* produced the following revelations:

- Following the phone advice from a police dispatcher (who said no police were available to assist him because it was Sunday) when he complained about a stray dog attacking his Doberman who was in heat, Gerardo Pici put the stray in his 1987 Mazda pickup truck (worth $11,000) and dropped the dog off in the woods a mile from his home. The next day Pinellas Park police (who were not available to assist Pici on Sunday) charged him with larceny of a dog and confiscated his truck.

- Acquitted by a Clearwater jury of the felonious assault of a police officer with his BMW car, William Zeig, a Tampa scientist who had equipped the car with a special $20,000 fuel injection engine, lost the engine and the car to forfeiture, even though he was freed of the charge on which the forfeiture was based.

- Even though acquitted of charges of theft, Pinellas Park police continued to press forfeiture against the truck owned by Steve Seligman, who had been accused wrongly of taking 10 sheets of construction steel. He lost his truck, $2,000 worth of tools it contained, and thousands in legal fees after his attorney explained that it would cost more than the truck was worth to fight the battle in court.

- When a Pinellas County circuit court judge ordered the return of Benito Marerro's Datsun 280Z after a plea bargain arrangement in a bad check case, the owner discovered the police had sold it to a salvage company a week before in spite of the pending forfeiture case. The car had been crushed into a ball of metal scrap. The police kept the money from the sale.

- The neighboring Tampa city police were the local forfeiture champions in 1988. With an attorney, two detectives, and a secretary working full time only on forfeitures, the Tampa police confiscated more than 900 motor vehicles allegedly used to commit felonies and obtained $206,330 in cash from their owners, who were forced to buy back their own cars in "settlements" with the police! All this without any adjudication of criminal conduct, or even any charges against the owners in most cases.

The Sheriff of Volusia County

One of the classic cases of police abuse of forfeiture powers occurred on a continuing basis in Volusia County (the Daytona Beach area) in northeast Florida, which sits astride Interstate 95, the major East Coast north-south auto and truck route to Miami and south Florida.

This scandal was first exposed in an investigative special report in the *Orlando Sentinel* in June 1992. Reporters Jeff Brazil and Steve Berry discovered that Volusia County Sheriff Bob Vogel had created a special police "drug squad" that literally preyed upon thousands of innocent motorists driving on I-95. Operating under the broadly written 1980 Florida Contraband Forfeiture Act, which allowed police seizure of cash and property based on "probable cause" without arrests in suspected felony cases, the police were engaging in what can charitably be called "highway robbery." Police conduct was guided by no written rules and reviewed by no one but Sheriff

Vogel, and he controlled all the funds confiscated. Any person stopped who possessed $100 or more in cash was to be assumed a drug trafficker under the sheriff's rules. The following are a few of the facts uncovered by the *Sentinel*:

- Less than 1 percent of the drivers were given traffic tickets, and only one in four were charged with any criminal conduct, usually involving drug offenses. In 1989 there were cash seizures from 83 percent of the people stopped, but only 19 percent were arrested for alleged crimes.

- From 1989 until the adverse publicity in 1992, the squad seized more than $8 million in cash from motorists—and in only four cases did the innocent owners get all their money back! In any of the cases where money was returned to motorists, the sheriff always kept a substantial amount (10 to 25 percent) for "expenses."

- It was regular police practice to bargain with motorists stopped on the side of I-95 on the spot—taking part (10 to 50 percent) of their cash in exchange for agreement not to file claims for the cash or to take legal action against the sheriff's department or the police. Some drivers were stripped of their cash because they "looked like" drug suspects—one because he had no luggage, another because he had "too much" luggage. Carrying U.S. currency in denominations that the sheriff's deputies felt were typical of drug dealers—including $1, $10, $20, $50, and $100 bills—also resulted in confiscation! And the police repeatedly used the discredited excuse that illegal drug residue was found on the currency confiscated—an irrelevant fact true of at least 80 to 90 percent of all U.S. paper money in circulation. It was standard practice for Volusia deputies to use a drug-sniffing dog to examine currency when a car was stopped, and the police told the unsuspecting driver that this was hard evidence that he or she was involved in illegal "drug" activities.

• Interestingly, the sheriff's "Selective Enforcement Team" rarely stopped vehicles traveling in the northbound lanes of I-95 (those most likely to be carrying quantities of drugs to northern cities from south Florida smuggling points). Instead, they concentrated on the southbound lanes, assuming this was where they would find people headed to south Florida to buy drugs with their easily forfeitable cash—which the police confiscated. So much for sincere concern about "interdiction" and winning the "war on drugs."

Often when car occupants were considered "suspicious" by deputies, they were told to wait in a police patrol car, where their conversation was secretly recorded by a hidden microphone. Because the suspects were not under arrest, the police read them no statements of their legal rights but used the slightest remark that could be interpreted as supporting forfeiture for possible drug trafficking to justify confiscation of their money.

ELSEWHERE IN AMERICA

Lest you think the Volusia County experience was a one-time aberration among law enforcement agencies, consider the case of Eagle County in the northwest corner of Colorado. There in the beautiful Rocky Mountains, a 70-mile stretch of Interstate 70 winds past Vail and other fashionable ski areas, and there, during 1989 and 1990, more than 500 drivers were stopped, primarily, as two deputies testified in a federal class action suit, because the drivers were black or Hispanic. The sheriff's office there also created a profile of "drug couriers" based on race, ethnicity, and out-of-state auto license plates. In ruling that this tactic was unconstitutional, U.S. District Court Judge Jim Carrigan said, "If this nation were to win its war on drugs at the cost of sacrificing its citizens' constitutional rights, it would be a Pyrrhic victory indeed. If the rule of law rather than the rule of man is to prevail, there cannot be one set of search and seizure rules applicable to some and a different set applicable to others."

On the West Coast

In the state of California, in its four years under a tough state forfeiture law (which was severely curtailed by the legislature in 1994), property confiscations produced a hefty $180 million for California police. But among the more than 16,000 forfeiture cases filed in the state since 1989, the *San Jose Mercury News*, in an extensive 1993 investigation, turned up numerous cases in the five counties surveyed in which property owner "victims" were never charged or convicted of any crime. Most who lost property to police seizure were not "drug lords" or "kingpins," but rather poor people who spoke little or no English, usually Latinos—in other words, those least able to defend themselves, thus ripe for the plucking. Interestingly, as forfeitures increased in each of the four years the old law was in effect, California drug arrests and convictions declined steadily. Confiscated illegal drugs are not worth much—property is.

The following is a sampling of the Golden State record on forfeitures that prompted reform:

- After Kay Van Sant's 30-year-old son was arrested on drug trafficking charges, the Bakersfield police went to her bank and drained her checking account of $3,912.00 in cash. A self-employed bookkeeper, she had not lived with her son for more than 10 years and she was never charged with any crime. She never got her money back.

- Robert De La Torres' pickup truck was seized after his cousin was arrested in it with a pound of marijuana. De La Torres, who speaks no English, tried to explain to a Kern County judge that he had loaned the truck to his cousin while he was on a trip to Mexico, but he never got a chance. Stating that "the court doesn't speak Spanish," the judge awarded the truck to the police, ignoring De La Torres' pleas for an interpreter.

- Former Los Angeles narcotics detective Robert R. Sobel, who headed one of the county's most productive anti-drug squads in the 1980s, testified in court that members of his task force routinely lied under oath, falsified police reports, invented fictitious informants, planted drugs, and beat suspects to get money and valuables from them. Twelve L.A. County police were convicted of crimes associated with this one drug unit.

- Attorney Robin Walters, who headed the Kern County forfeiture unit for two years, saw a distinct change in that time. "Police and prosecutors," he said, "have gone crazy with this law. They're rabid. They'll take anything, whether it has anything to do with drugs or not, because they know most people will never be able to get it back."

- Sacramento attorney Phil Cozens, a former prosecutor, described the discriminating attitude the police displayed when they raided a client's apartment as follows: "They took a bottle of LaFitte Rothschild 1984, but strangely enough, they left a bottle of Dom Perignon 1982. They took some very bizarre red wines and left most champagnes and whites." In other raids police took a full set of auto tires, a child's Nintendo game, an antique belt buckle, and a jar of pennies. And, in the case of the L.A. County Sheriff's Department drug unit, they took tens of millions of dollars.

- The *Los Angeles Times* reported in January 1992 that six L.A. County Sheriff's narcotics officers went to trial on charges of "stealing hundreds of thousands of dollars in cash and property during drug raids, beating suspects, planting narcotics, and falsifying police reports." In another trial in March 1992, two other of the same department's narcotics officers were charged with drug money skimming, and the *Times* reported that Deputy Sheriff Eufasio G. Cortez testified that the money skimming scandal began " . . . with narcotics officers taking 'a few dollars off the top' to buy law enforcement equipment or dinner after a successful drug raid but quickly spread out of control. Narcotics officers began stealing seized property including television sets, stereos, and jewelry that had been confiscated during raids. . . . Before long officers were skimming hundreds, then thousands of dollars in cash."

Ten of the L.A. County officers were convicted of various charges, and five were either acquitted or subjects of mistrials on some counts. A former L.A. sheriff's deputy, Robert Sobel, who was indicted and turned state's evidence, testified that his narcotics unit stole $60 million in cash and property during 1988 and 1989 alone.

• In 1992 *The Washington Post* and local station WRC-TV reported on a major scandal in the Washington, D.C. Police Department involving confiscated firearms. (Possession of any firearms in the District of Columbia is illegal.) It seems that the Police Property Clerk's office, charged with keeping all seized guns under lock and key, was missing 2,864 confiscated weapons, two of which turned up as murder weapons in other crimes. The guns were kept in unsealed boxes, police employees were the only ones controlling the inventory, and the storage area doubled as a lunch room. There were also numerous reports of police stopping suspects on the street, confiscating any cash found on them, then not reporting the forfeiture. In 1987 Effie Barry, the wife of then Washington Mayor Marion Barry, was exposed as driving around in a Lincoln Town Car forfeited from an accused criminal. D.C. government officials defended this use as "government service." It has also been a Washington police practice to seize autos of men accused of soliciting for prostitution, and the cars are forfeited, even if the "johns" are acquitted. Arrests are usually made by undercover street "decoys" who are policewomen.

CHAPTER

3

Federal Forfeiture Law

Throughout American history (at least until the inception of the current "war on drugs"), government forfeiture of property was a highly unpopular concept, principally because forfeiture was widely abused by the British Crown in its attempt to tax, control, and punish American colonists. "Writs of assistance" and "general warrants" were both British legal devices allowing the Royal Navy to search colonial American ships and to seize and forfeit them. The King's officers were particularly arrogant and arbitrary with American colonists when seizing property for forfeiture, and Americans accused of tax or customs duty evasion were remanded to special admiralty courts outside the regular judicial framework that was supported by domestic taxation. The admiralty courts conducted trials by Crown officers whose pay and expenses came wholly from the fines and forfeitures that they adjudged. Jury trials were denied, and colonial protests against the basic conflict of interest of such a system were ignored.

This early American distrust of asset forfeiture is reflected not only in the property protection afforded by the due process clause in the Fifth Amendment to the Constitution, but also in a specific limitation on forfeiture as a punishment for treason in Article III, which states the following:

> Congress shall have the power to declare the punishment for treason, but no attainder of treason shall work corruption of blood, or forfeiture except during the life of the person attainted.

Similarly, British law provided for the seizure of felons' estates, a practice the first U.S. Congress forbade by the Act of April 30, 1790, which remains the law today.

Nevertheless, forfeiture did find some use in the early United States, and the first Congress adopted several maritime forfeiture laws restricted to admiralty matters and as civil sanctions against ships and cargo for failure to pay customs duties. The U.S. Supreme Court generally upheld these early admiralty and customs forfeiture laws.

Why did Americans adopt English admiralty law, notwithstanding our rightful sensitivity to English barbarisms, especially property forfeiture? The reason for even a limited embrace was simple—government's eternal need for money. In the early years of our republic, before federal income taxes were even a bad dream, import duties constituted more than 80 percent of all federal revenues.

During the Civil War, forfeiture was used by President Abraham Lincoln's government to confiscate the property of both Confederate rebels and their sympathizers. When Congress passed the Confiscation Act on July 17, 1862, authorizing *in rem* procedures against rebel property, the Supreme Court upheld it as part of broad military powers, stating, "The power to declare war involves the power to prosecute it by all means and in any manner in which war may be legitimately prosecuted. It therefore includes the right to seize and confiscate all property of the enemy and dispose of it at the will of the captor."

It is noteworthy that the Court upheld the law only because

it was a war powers exercise aimed at enemies of the Union; the justices unanimously stated that if the purposes of the Confiscation Act was to punish an individual for treason or other criminal offenses, it would be unconstitutional because it substituted *in rem* civil procedures for a criminal trial, which would afford a defendant the protections of the Fifth and Sixth Amendments. The majority said since the purpose was not to hold a person criminally liable but to speed the end of the Civil War, "the provisions made to carry out the purpose, viz., confiscation, were legitimate, unless applied to others than enemies." A few years later the Supreme Court restated this view, holding that if forfeiture of property, even though civil in nature, was actually based on offenses committed by the accused owner, the defendant is entitled to protections against self-incrimination and illegally obtained evidence that would apply in a criminal trial.

During the Prohibition era in America from 1919 to 1933, Congress extended civil asset forfeiture to include criminal violations of the Volstead Act and other laws governing the production, importation, and consumption of alcoholic beverages, although forfeiture was limited to those portions of real property actually used for moonshine production. In 1921 the Supreme Court upheld the forfeiture of an auto dealer's secured interest in a vehicle used to transport moonshine, even though the car had been sold to a bona fide purchaser and the dealer had no involvement in the crime.

THE WAR ON DRUGS

It is in this historic context that we arrive at the full flowering of civil asset forfeiture in America: the war to banish what lawmakers have chosen to call "controlled dangerous substances," i.e., drugs or other substances, the manufacture, distribution, or possession of which have been made illegal by act of Congress or state legislatures.

As we have seen, forfeiture was rarely used in America until the 1980s, but since then it has flourished, first as a weapon in the arsenal of the drug war, and more recently in combating a host of criminal acts. In fact, during the first 10 years that federal drug forfeiture powers were available, law enforcement officials rarely used them. This lack of use prompted the General Accounting Office to issue a 1981 report entitled "Asset Forfeiture—A Seldom Used Tool in Combating Drug Trafficking," which was instrumental in speeding up the volume and scope of property confiscation. Congress soon joined the forfeiture game with gusto.

The Comprehensive Drug Abuse Prevention and Control Act of 1970 contains the basic federal antidrug civil asset forfeiture provisions that provide for "the forfeiture of all controlled substances which have been manufactured, distributed, dispensed, or acquired and all raw materials, products, and equipment . . . which are used, or intended for use, in manufacturing . . . delivering, importing, or exporting controlled substances . . . property which is used, or intended for use, as a container for forfeitable controlled substances . . . all conveyances, including aircraft, vehicles, or vessels, which are used, or intended for use, to transport, or in any manner to facilitate the transportation, sale, receipt, possession or concealment [of such controlled substances."

In 1978, the act was amended to provide for forfeiture of the following:

"all moneys . . . or other things of value furnished or intended to be furnished by any person in exchange for a controlled substance . . . all proceeds traceable to such an exchange."

In 1984, the act was again amended to provide for forfeiture of "all real property . . . which is used, or intended to be used, in any manner or part, to commit, or to facilitate the commission of a violation . . ."

Contained in this review of congressional action is an important political progression of legislative events, which a prudent investor must recognize. The 1970 Comprehensive Drug Abuse Prevention and Control Act provided for the forfeiture of property used in connection with controlled substances. The 1978 Psychotropic Substances Act added forfeiture of money and other things of value furnished or intended to be furnished in exchange for a controlled substance and all proceeds traceable to such an exchange. The 1984 Comprehensive Crime Control Act added all real property used or intended to be used to commit or to facilitate the commission of a drug crime. The 1986 Anti-Drug Abuse Act expanded civil forfeiture to include the proceeds of "money laun-dering" activity.

Certain 1990 amendments to that act went beyond drug activ-ity and included forfeiture of proceeds traceable to counterfeiting and other offenses affecting financial institutions—a congressional bow to the savings and loan scandals. Again in 1992, Congress added more categories of offenses and included forfeiture of cash proceeds traceable to motor vehicle theft.

Perhaps the most dramatic departure from basic drug forfeiture law came in 1992 with the adoption of a statute that applies "in any forfeiture *in rem* in which the subject property is cash, monetary instruments in bearer form, funds deposited in an account in a financial institution . . . or other fungible property."

Under this provision, the government does not have to iden-tify the specific property (or cash) involved in the offense that is the basis for forfeiture but may seize "any identical property found in the same place or the same account as the property involved in the offense," which might have been forfeitable had it remained in the same place or account. That means that even though tainted cash may have been spent or transferred elsewhere, any cash available belonging to the same owner can be snatched by the feds in its stead. The Justice Department has even argued in court that the deposit of $1 in illicit criminal money makes the entire amount deposited in the account "tainted" and open to forfeiture. Remember, we are not talking only about "drug money," but any cash, negotiable instruments, or commodities (gold for instance), that police may relate to numerous acts of alleged criminal conduct prohibited by statute. And the owner of the cash or account holder need not be charged with a crime in order for the money to be con-fiscated by police.

All this statutory forfeiture expansion means not only a dra-matic increase in the number of crimes covered by civil asset forfei-ture, but also a significant lessening of any relationship between an alleged guilty act or offense and the property that is subjected to for-feiture. The implications of this property "guilt by association" trend are enormous for investors and their property.

THE "RICO" LAW

Take, for example, the federal antiracketeering law, the Racketeering and Corrupt Organizations Act, which contains punitive criminal forfeiture provisions. The courts have had no hesitation in applying RICO's broad criminal (as compared to civil) forfeiture language in order to curb the power of criminals over American business. The law has allowed the seizure of both illegitimately and legally acquired assets as punishment, but only after a defendant has been charged, tried, and convicted of a crime, presumably with the protection of all due process guarantees, including a trial by jury. In the sense that noncriminally acquired assets can be forfeited as punishment under RICO, this use of criminal forfeiture is in some respects potentially even broader in scope than civil forfeiture.

Investors and businesspeople should be troubled by the breadth of RICO application allowed by some courts. Under RICO, for example, a convicted defendant must forfeit *any* property interest, however legitimately it may have been acquired or employed, if that interest allows the defendant to exercise a source of influence over an alleged RICO "enterprise," which now has become a very broadly interpreted term—so much so that it has been held to encompass peaceful picketing by antiabortion protesters at abortion clinics.

Going after Business

This liberal view of RICO's scope taken together with asset forfeiture has the potential for far-reaching and dangerous consequences of many types. Although secondary to a loss of individual liberty, forfeiture actions against any property can and does cause serious disruption to commercial life affecting the rights of those having nothing to do with alleged criminal acts. A New York RICO defendant convicted of failure to pay a state sales tax due from his gas station franchise was ordered to forfeit not only an amount equal to what he owed in delinquent taxes and penalties, but also to forfeit 29 separate corporations through which he legally owned and operated a chain of gas stations.

Once an offending use is made of property, under the theory of civil forfeiture, title to that property *immediately* passes to the gov-

ernment! Until the Supreme Court in 1993 approved some limitations on this theory in *United States v. 92 Buena Vista Ave.*, 113
S.Ct. 1126 (1993), subsequent innocent purchasers of the so-called
"tainted property" could have it confiscated at any time, regardless
of the buyer's lack of knowledge about the alleged illegal prior use.
Similarly, unsecured creditors, lenders, mechanics, and suppliers can
lose their valuable interests in such properties with little or no
recourse for payment.

Exactly this scenario occurred in the case of a New York
financier accused by the Department of Justice of business fraud by
obtaining large bank loans secured by false statements of automobile
inventory. In *United States v. McNamara Buick-Pontiac*, No. CV-92-
2070 (EDNY 1992), the government sought forfeiture of the
owner's $400 million corporate empire, including a car dealership,
real estate holdings, a gold mine, and many other legitimate enterprises, with no regard for the unsecured rights of numerous creditors
who were owed millions of dollars for legitimate goods and services
rendered to the accused's businesses prior to government seizure.
The McNamara case is, so far, the third largest federal civil forfeiture case, the only larger ones involving "junk bond king" Michael
Milken's forfeiture of $900 million to the SEC for defrauded
investors, and the Bank of Commerce and Credit International
(BCCI) forfeiture of $500 million to defrauded U.S. depositors.

File Your CTRs or Else

RICO is not the only basis for government forfeiture attacks
on business. In January 1993, in what was obviously a high-profile
government sting operation, the real and personal business property (including an auto inventory worth more than $2.5 million) of 11
auto sales dealerships in the Maryland and Virginia suburbs of
Washington, D.C., were seized by federal authorities after 19 sales-
people were charged with accepting cash in excess of $10,000 for
auto purchases made by undercover police. There was no allegation
of drug money being used or any tax evasion by the dealerships, only
that they failed to file "currency transaction reports" (CTRs) with
the U.S. Internal Revenue Service for cash transactions involving
$10,000 or more, as required under the Money Laundering Control

Act of 1986. Under that law, there is no requirement that any of the funds be in any way involved in criminal activity—the crime occurs when there is a failure to report the cash transfer to the IRS. Penalties under the act include a mandatory five-year prison term, a $250,000 fine, and forfeiture of any funds involved.

Under penalty of forfeiture you also must file a CTR if you buy more than $3,000 in money orders or make cash transfers among your bank accounts in a series totaling more than $10,000, known in government jargon as "structuring" your cash assets. In 1991 a New Jersey homeowner refinanced his home to provide for his son's college education and to pay accumulated personal bills, receiving a cashier's check for $38,000 from his bank. He then withdrew $15,000 of these funds and purchased several postal money orders, depositing them by mail in his son's custodial account in a Maryland bank where his son was attending college. A few weeks later U.S. Postal Service inspectors seized the Maryland bank account, alleging violations of money structuring and failure to report cash transfers—laws about which the hapless homeowner knew nothing and about which the postal clerks failed to inform him. When his attorney filed a petition with the Department of Justice to get the money back, it was denied on the grounds that the father failed to show he was ignorant of the reporting law.

Right to Counsel Impaired

A similar but equally serious constitutional problem has arisen in the area of criminal forfeiture based on RICO and the Drug Kingpin Statute, both of which allow courts to issue pretrial asset retraining orders. Such "freeze" orders prevent a criminal defendant from transferring or even using his assets prior to trial. Such pretrial orders have great utility in criminal actions for prosecutors because the government has no legal right to seize any assets until after conviction at trial, which may require several years. (In a civil forfeiture case the government's right to seize the property is immediate and in theory arises at the instant the alleged criminal use of the property occurs.)

There is an obvious constitutional problem here because, as a nation of laws, we must accord every accused defendant the presumption of innocence until proven guilty. But a pretrial freeze order can tie up an accused's ability to pay living expenses and attorneys' fees, thus impairing his right to obtain legal counsel of his choosing. In a remarkable case in 1989, the Supreme Court actually upheld the pretrial use of criminal forfeiture laws that prevented the defendant from paying for his defense counsel. In so doing, the Court conjured up a rationale which seems to have little basis in any congressional intent. It held that criminal forfeiture could act not only as a sanction for criminal acts but also as a revenue-raising mechanism for the Department of Justice to finance restitution for crime victims—a program that the government has never claimed existed nor implemented in actual practice.

LAW FIRMS ANOTHER TARGET

In March 1992 the SEC, which had filed suit against the prestigious national law firm of Kaye, Scholer, Fierman, Hays & Handler, froze all the assets of the firm, which represented Lincoln Federal Savings and Loan and its former president Charles Keating, who was convicted of fraud. Claiming the law firm had concealed information about its clients from its investigators, the SEC sought $275 million in fines. Even though the SEC had sued the law firm, the government did not go to court to seek an order or any hearing on the merits of the seizure of the law firm's assets, which instantly destroyed the firm's ability to operate, meet payrolls, or even write a check. The firm's clients began calling to cancel their representation. Unable to conduct business, the management of the law firm settled with the SEC in a few days for $41 million in fines. All this occurred without any access to a judicial forum or any due process of law as usually understood. The *New York Law Journal* commented that "the government's use of a tactic as bare-fisted as the freeze order left many lawyers fearing for their profession's future" (not to mention what it implies about the long-cherished right to counsel and the attorney-client privilege).

There is even reason to believe that prosecutors and police are using forfeiture in an attempt to intimidate and coerce lawyers prominent in the criminal defense bar in order to set an example to other lawyers.

On March 31, 1992, while California attorney Terry Fields was at work, federal agents seized his $3 million Malibu home where he had his family had lived for three years. They justified their action on the grounds that Fields had received the house as payment for legal services he rendered to a criminal defendant.

On the night of August 6, 1993, a highly respected San Francisco criminal lawyer and civic leader, Patrick Hallinan, was arrested at gunpoint in his home, which was surrounded by DEA agents. He was charged with drug smuggling and money laundering based on accusations made by his former client, convicted drug kingpin Ciro Mancuso, already sentenced to life in prison after a 1990 guilty plea in which he agreed to cooperate with federal prosecutors. Another attorney in Reno, Nevada, and 40 other codefendants were also arrested. It appears Hallinan's arrest was purposely made on a Friday evening when no federal magistrate was available to set bail so Hallinan could be forced to spend the weekend in jail. He was physically injured by federal agents, who pushed him upstairs while his hands were handcuffed behind him. It was reported that Mancuso's family was getting back his property previously forfeited to the federal government in return for his informing on those he accused.

In both of these California cases involving lawyers, the federal government is seeking not only to forfeit the attorneys' homes, but also their entire law firms and the firms' assets—a first in America. The National Association of Criminal Defense Lawyers denounced the unprecedented seizing of the law firms. Observers pointed out that this was probably meant to intimidate a wider audience of criminal attorneys, since the law firm would be worthless to the government without the lawyers, who, if convicted, would lose their licenses to practice law in any event.

ANCIENT PROCEDURES

The fact that government forfeiture has been justified by the modern war on drugs notwithstanding, a distinctly American asset forfeiture policy has mushroomed, far removed from any English common law notion of "arresting," "guilty," or "tainted" property "accused" of causing a wrong. And yet for the most part, the original common law judicial procedures used for forfeitures govern this whole new federal apparatus of criminal acts, often much to the detriment of individual constitutional rights and the delight of those in and out of government who benefit from wholesale confiscation of billions of dollars worth of private property.

Current civil forfeiture law provides a most unsatisfactory approach to resolving claims by property owners affected by a forfeiture action. If you consider yourself to be an innocent owner whose property has been seized by the federal government, you may file a proof of your claim with the U.S. District Court. In such a case the validity of a claim will eventually be decided by a special trustee based on applicable statutory and common law, which means many of the legal problems described here will confront the claimant and his or her attorney—assuming the person can afford to challenge the government at all. A standard attorney's retainer fee in such a case starts at $10,000.

To the extent that a person seeking to make a claim on the forfeited property is not an "innocent owner"—including third party creditors or lien holders whose claims may be "innocent" but are based on financing or work or services rendered concerning the property—he may be out in the cold. Current law says such persons have no recognizable claim on the property, but—lucky them—they can petition the Department of Justice (as did the father who bought the money orders for his son's account) for an equitable remedy, which the Department of Justice, without a hearing—in its sole discretion, unreviewable on its merits in any court—may or may not grant as it sees fit. Unlike the federal bankruptcy law with two centuries of statutory and case-developed procedures, where creditors and lien holders are allowed to participate, forfeiture claimants are left to the tender mercy of an administrative petition procedure from which there is no recourse. Once the claimant chooses this petition route, he loses all recourse to the courts.

This inequitable arrangement places the decision on return of the property or payment of claims in the hands of the very agency that stands to profit from its retention and from denial of any and all claims. In an increasingly complex commercial world, such a Rube Goldberg system to handle valid claims against forfeited property invites—nay, in fact guarantees—inequity and business disaster.

The "Personification" Fiction

Perhaps the most persistent rationale behind federal forfeiture statutory and case law is the "personification" fiction—"the thing is primarily considered the offender." Civil asset forfeiture is premised on an archaic and curious legal fiction that personifies property. This "personification theory" holds that an object can commit a wrong and be held guilty for its misdeeds. Therefore, it is argued, property may be subject to punishment. That punishment is forfeiture.

The glorification and unquestioning acceptance by the courts of this primitive legal fiction (and its numerous associated fictions) always has been at the heart of the forfeiture problem. Property owners whose assets have been seized often try to press their claims for relief through traditional, well-respected legal arguments, such as their not having been accused of criminal conduct, their right to be presumed innocent, or the fact that the government has taken their property without affording them any notice or hearing as required by due process.

Unfortunately, those formidable legal arguments that normally would succeed have, until very recently, proved unavailing. Instead, an otherwise rational judge informs the property owner that it is the property, not him or her, that is being prosecuted by the government; that in the eyes of the government, the property is a criminal perpetrator; and that it is the property's rights (or lack thereof), not those of its human owner, that determine the sufficiency of the procedures the government can use to confiscate. More than one property owner has been baffled by this Alice in Wonderland spectacle, even when his or her lawyer tries to explain.

Small wonder that with forfeiture as their hunting license, law enforcement agencies have been raiding lucrative "cookie jars" with appalling abandon. This has been allowed for two very crude tactical reasons on the part of government: the personification ruse disarms private property owners of their rights and defenses, even as it eases the way for law enforcement to confiscate property unrestrained by the usual rules of due process. In fact, in the vast majority of asset forfeiture cases the property owner is not even charged with a crime, yet the government officials can—and usually do—keep the seized property.

Procedural due process, guaranteed by the Fifth and Fourteenth Amendments to the Constitution, is totally lacking in asset forfeiture cases. Instead, the judicial system is stacked against the innocent citizen and in favor of government. The property owner, if indigent, is entitled to no appointed attorney, must post a 10-percent cash bond based on the value of the property seized for the privilege of contesting the government's action, and is allowed only days to file a claim or lose that right. And even if the owner is successful, the government is not liable for damage to the property or for storage or other charges. As the *Chicago Tribune* editorially stated on April 1, 1993, "A growing number of innocent parties . . . are being swept up in the net (of forfeiture). And those who are unfairly trapped find that forfeiture laws turn due process on its head."

To justify its seizure of property, whether it be your wallet or your house, government need only present evidence of what its agents see as "probable cause," the same feeble legal standard normally required to obtain a search warrant, a legal document that only allows police to seek evidence of crime, not permanently take your property. Even worse, under asset forfeiture the greater burden of proof is imposed on the property owner, who must establish by a "preponderance of the evidence" that his or her property has not been used in a criminal act. Once a government agent shows a court he had "probable cause" to take your property, the government keeps it without need of any further justification, whether or not a crime was committed by you or anyone else. Often "probable cause" is mere rumor, gossip, a police hunch, or self-serving statements from anonymous paid police informants, criminals cooperating in order to obtain a lighter sentence on a pending charge, or from incarcerated convicts trying to shorten an existing jail term.

At the urging of the Justice Department during the 1980s, federal courts adopted probable cause as the majority evidentiary rule in forfeiture cases—acceptable proof on which to base government taking of property. This occurred in spite of the universal legal knowl-

edge that probable cause can be established by little more than rank
hearsay, gossip, or rumor. Here's how it operates: one person says to
another, "That guy, Smith, looks like he does drugs." An informant
overhears this idle gossip and reports it to the police, who in turn
seize Smith's residence and start forfeiture proceedings. No drugs are
found, and Smith is never arrested or charged with a crime. Yet
Smith is forced to hire a lawyer and fight in court to get his house
back—and he and his family may well have been evicted from their
home. Sometimes the government will kindly allow the Smith family to stay on in their own home, if they agree to pay rent to the feds.

You may think this sounds farfetched, but the Justice
Department has even argued in court that the test for forfeiture
probable cause can be met when a law enforcement officer simply
repeats an anonymous informant's tip—"he said that she said."

What "Probable Cause" Means

In practical terms what does the use of "probable cause" mean
in the life of an owner or investor whose property stands accused?

In Connecticut, a man named Bobby Watts was arrested for
growing large quantities of marijuana on his farm. Facing a 38-year
prison sentence, he was offered a deal by federal prosecutors: "turn
in other pot growers and we'll go easy on you." The obliging Watts
told U.S. prosecutors in New Haven that a couple named Cwiklas
had 300 pounds of pot stored in their residence. (Later Watts' story
dwindled down to 200, 100—then only one pound of pot.) In
exchange for this tale, Watts got a suspended sentence and his farm
was not forfeited as it might have been. When another informant
was asked to corroborate Watt's accusations against the Cwiklas, he
failed a lie detector test in doing so.

Without any other verification of these serious accusations,
and without searching the house first, Assistant U.S. Attorney
Leslie Ohta filed forfeiture proceedings and confiscated the Cwiklas'
residence. No pot was found, and they were not charged with any
crime. But the Cwiklas were forced to go into U.S. District Court to
try and get their home returned.

There you see the practical meaning of "probable cause" supported by "hearsay" evidence.

It is worth noting that Assistant U.S. Attorney Ohta had gained quite a public name for herself as a result of her aggressive pursuit of forfeitures, taking the homes of parents and even grandparents whose children or grandchildren used, sold, or stored pot in the homes, even though without the homeowners' knowledge or consent. She insisted that such hapless relatives had a positive duty to know at all times what their offspring were doing, even in the privacy of their rooms.

As fate would have it, in December 1989, Ohta's son was arrested for possession of marijuana and selling LSD out of *her* car. Court papers revealed that an undercover police agent also had bought pot from Ohta's son in his parent's home in Glastonbury. Unlike her many forfeiture victims, Ohta was allowed by her cronies at the Justice Department to keep her car and her home, but she was removed from forfeiture cases—too late to be of any help to the hapless Cwiklas who had lost their home through the official cooperation of informant Watts and attorney Ohta. In a final irony, Ohta was reassigned by the Justice Department to train other U.S. attorneys on how to conduct forfeiture cases!

Prove Your Innocence

The basic American presumption of innocence until proven guilty has not only been reversed, but property owners are now being forced to show evidence of their innocence by serving as police agents expected to incriminate others. Property of innocent owners can be taken unless the owners can prove not only that alleged illegal activity on the premises occurred without their knowledge or consent but that they did all that "reasonably could be expected to prevent the proscribed use of the property." Think what this could mean to you. If your teenager is allowed to use the family car and police find a marijuana "roach" discarded by one of your child's passengers, it could mean good-bye to your BMW. Property owners who lease apartments, cars, or boats risk losing their valuable property because of renters' conduct over which the innocent owner has, and can have, no control. How can a landlord ever know which tenants in any apartment building may smoke pot, gamble at card games, or use an illegal TV descrambler? And what can they do about it if they do know?

The onus should be placed on the government to show guilty knowledge and lack of consent on the part of an owner in order to deprive that person of his or her property. There is an obvious inherent difficulty in trying to prove a negative proposition, i.e., when an owner must adduce that he or she did not know something or did not consent to something. This is especially difficult when an owner must counter anonymous government informers (or even police) who are ready and willing to say almost anything to support forfeiture.

Along with those guilty criminals who deserve to lose their property, many innocent people indeed have been gravely injured by the application of forfeiture laws—including Karen Lavallee of Burlington, Vermont, and her three young children, ages 6, 9, and 11. Her husband was convicted in Minnesota for trafficking cocaine and went to prison for 10 years. Federal authorities seized the Vermont family home and evicted Karen and her children, who were forced to go on welfare. "I don't condone what my husband did, but why victimize my children because of his actions?" she asked. So many cases of this nature occurred in Vermont that a grassroots group was formed called Stop Forfeiture of Children's Homes.

It was because of just such cruel results as that experienced by Karen Lavallee and her children that Congress and many of the individual states amended traditional civil forfeiture laws by creating exemptions for innocent property owners. That compassionate action embodies a principle that judges, legislators, and law enforcement officials should always keep in mind when considering this topic: innocent people should not suffer property loss simply because of broad forfeiture statutes.

These "innocent owner" exceptions notwithstanding, in many jurisdictions proof of "innocence" requires a great deal more than showing that a property owner is not a criminal.

The innocent owner must prove that he lacked both knowledge of and control over the property's lawful use. Thus civil forfeiture not only makes a property owner his brother's keeper but compels him to prevent the unlawful use of his property by his brother— or anyone else for that matter. This situation only exacerbates the disparity in the law's treatment of the criminally accused and the nonaccused property owner. To obtain a criminal forfeiture, the government must prove a defendant's intentional criminal conduct.

By contrast, to be exempt from civil seizure and forfeiture, a property owner must prove a negative: that is, he must prove he lacked any knowledge (*mens rea*) of the property's unlawful use, even though mere knowledge of criminal conduct is typically insufficient to establish criminal culpability under criminal law.

Numerous federal courts, at the urging of the Justice Department, have seriously eroded the statutory innocent owner protections by ruling that an owner must pass the following three-part test: 1) prove he or she had no knowledge of the illegal use (and was not "willfully blind" to such use); 2) did not consent to the prohibited use; and 3) took all reasonable steps available to prevent it. This constitutes a very difficult, if not impossible, burden of proof.

Urban Renewal by Forfeiture

There are some very compelling reasons for the innocent owner exemption in federal law. In some areas of the country law enforcement authorities have revealed plans to confiscate real property on a wholesale basis as part of the war on drugs. For example, in Colorado in 1992, Denver police seized three motels in a ghetto area long plagued by drug trafficking. Denver police Lt. Jerry Frazzini told the *Rocky Mountain News*, "If necessary it [seizures of property] will continue until the city owns the whole corridor." This may sound at first blush a good way to combat open air drug markets, but the implications of such a policy are horrendous. This kind of blatant drug activity occurs in older, poorer neighborhoods where property owners have little or no control over drug trafficking and most fervently wish the police did have some control. When police "sweeps" occur, drug pushers move a block or two away, thus endangering more private property as possible objects of forfeiture.

The potential for government abuse, absent a strong innocent owner defense, is enormous, especially taken together with the "relation back theory" and the "taint" doctrine, which generally state that title to real property vests in the government from the moment criminal conduct occurs within its boundaries. Such a policy could mean government taking of large tracts of inner city real estate without just payment or any compensation—surely a cruel blow to many innocent people, many of them members of the minority community. And a land grab described as part of the war against drugs would be great official cover if a city wanted to build a freeway off ramp (or any public works) without paying land acquisition costs.

All this means that real estate investors, brokers, and management firms must realize that it's only a matter of time until one of the properties in which they have an interest or they manage is seized for drug activity. Neither the property owner nor the management company may have the financial standing to defend against forfeiture, and when the owner loses, he will probably seek legal redress against the on-site management company based on a lack of vigilance. The implied cost and legal ramifications are endless. Just consider what publicity about such forfeitures can do to the real estate market and property values in any affected area.

Structured Steering

So attractive has the forfeiture of valuable real estate become to police that most departments have quietly adopted a policy of "structured arrests," or "steering," making certain that undercover agents purchase drugs or make deals when they are physically located in a valuable building or on a high-priced tract of land—which immediately after the "buy" can be confiscated by the police. The use of even a small part of a larger parcel of land as the focus of an alleged drug crime can render the entire tract subject to forfeiture, under the theory that the use of the land "facilitates" the commission of the crime. Thus the use of a car parked in a driveway in which the purchase of cocaine occurred rendered the entire house and land subject to forfeiture. And when a drug transaction took place in an area including a driveway, house, and swimming pool, the government could seize all that area and 30 acres of land adjoining as well.

No Rest in Peace under Forfeiture

Not even the dead can escape possible real estate forfeiture, apparently. Three months before he died of cancer at the age of 49, wealthy George Gerhardt, who had no criminal record, was the subject of a secret police informant's juicy tip. The tipster claimed Gerhardt was paid $10,000 for the use of the boat dock at his $250,000 Fort Lauderdale, Florida, waterfront home where the informant said cocaine shipments from South America were unloaded. However, the informant could not recall the name of the boat, the date it happened, or even the dealers' names, and thus the government's legal brief stated it "does not possess the facts necessary to be more specific." Six months after he died, Gerhardt's heirs, who had inherited the family home, were ousted from the premises, the locks were changed, and the government rented it out for $2,200 a month. No warrant was ever issued for anyone's arrest, no charges were made against any living person, and, on the basis of a secret informer, the house was taken. Assistant U.S. Attorney for the Southern District of Florida, Robyn Hermann, admitted the obvious: the purpose was "not so much to punish at this stage. The motivation is really to use the proceeds from the sale of the property to prevent other drug offenses." Fortunately, in 1993 a U.S. district judge overturned the forfeiture, ruling that the heirs were entitled to a hearing before confiscation could be allowed (which isn't to say that the forfeiture won't eventually be allowed).

Government Vandalism

You should know that in federal forfeiture cases, if a property owner is lucky enough subsequently to recover his or her business, home, car, or boat, he or she often receives it back in a severely damaged condition. Vacant and boarded-up real property is especially subject to deterioration. And many times, as in the case of Professor Klein's yacht in Florida, government agents utterly destroy property in futile searches for contraband. It has long been the practice of U.S. Customs agents to use chainsaws to rip apart imported packages or objects in a hunt for contraband. Customs, short on staff, found this method attractive and efficient because they never have to compensate anyone for the damage they inflict. A report of the Committee on Ways and Means of the U.S. House of Representatives concluded, "The U.S. Customs Service has little or no incentive to avoid damaging cargo during examinations."

Many thousands of dollars of repairs are often necessary, and yet the federal government will not pay any damages because the Federal Tort Claims Act exempts government agencies from any claims arising from the detention of "goods or merchandise" by Customs or law enforcement officers. The General Accounting Office, the investigative arm of Congress, has repeatedly issued reports (nine in the last 10 years) detailing the sloppy, even irresponsible way in which federal agencies allow confiscated property to be damaged, stolen, or misused.

As the GAO notes, property awaiting forfeiture often devalues greatly: "Seized conveyances devalue from aging, lack of care, inadequate storage, and other factors while awaiting forfeiture. They often deteriorate—engines freeze, batteries die, seals shrink and leak oil, boats sink, salt air and water corrode metal surfaces, barnacles accumulate on boat hulls, and windows crack from heat. On occasion, vandals steal or seriously damage conveyances." Surely forfeiture law should—but doesn't—allow owners to sue the government for any damages to seized property caused by its agents or employees, so that blameless citizens can be made whole.

Informer's Paradise

Surely few (if any) American citizens could obtain joy from having to compare what goes on in the United States these days to what once was official policy in Adolf Hitler's Nazi Germany or Josef Stalin's late and unlamented Soviet Union. Both of these notorious totalitarian dictators sought to crush the spirit of human freedom by systematically destroying internal "enemies" and controlling the bodies (if not the minds and hearts) of the people. Central to the success of the Nazi and Communist police states was the care and feeding of a vast army of secret informers—Gestapo and KGB snitches who ratted to the police on their fellow citizens for pay, or just for spite.

History now repeats itself. One of the central pillars on which rests the dubious financial success of the federal forfeiture program is a similar army of well-paid secret informers—but with a big difference. In America, forfeiture informers, like personal injury lawyers, are paid on a contingency basis; the total amount and dollar value of the property they finger for successful forfeiture determines how much money the government pays into their personal bank accounts.

And what a great free enterprise incentive this has turned out to be for the motley crew of drug pushers, ex-cons, convicts, and other social misfits who have the questionable qualifications required for such grubby work. It is true that some few informers are merely patriotic citizens concerned about the welfare of their nation and the future of their children, those who perhaps stumble upon some bit of information useful to the police in tracking down crooks. And some, like that airline ticket agent in Nashville, are eager and willing to be used by the police because they want the extra money and it is an easy buck turning in black people who buy tickets with cash. At Denver's Stapleton Airport, where most drug investigations start with employees' tips, more than 2,000 people were detained for police questioning in 1991, yet there were only 49 arrests. One airline ticket clerk for a 12-month period was paid $5,834 by the U.S. Treasury and Denver County.

Informants, by their very nature, are not normal, gainfully employed, honest, upright citizens. They usually are, or have been, involved in drug or other serious criminal activity, and their motivation is to save their own skins or make money by selling information to the police. With criminal backgrounds and a personal stake in the outcome of a forfeiture case (25 percent of the value of the property), paid informants have strong incentives to lie, and they do.

Informants are totally insulated from any problems arising from their illicit activity; the property owner has no right to confront a secret witness in a civil asset forfeiture trial, and so informants need not risk public exposure by testifying—instead a police officer repeats what the informant told him. Most people never find out who accused their property of involvement in wrongdoing.

In 1990 and 1991 the Justice Department paid out more then $30 million to these informers, with a like amount budgeted for 1993. The Justice Department forfeiture chief in the Bush administration, Cary Copeland, in 1992 defended these expenditures as money well spent, saying, "We're not paying them because we like them. We're paying them because they put money in the pot." He estimated informers were responsible for as much as $130 million in forfeited cash flowing to federal coffers. Only a few days later it was reported in a *Washington Post* column that the highest paid federal informant in 1990 was compensated in the amount of $780,018.39 in a one-year period—more than the combined salary of both the president and vice president of the United States. The same *Post* column described the high life of "a typical informant" who had worked with government agents since 1988 while dealing drugs on the side. Several times he was caught in drug deals by other police unaware of his federal connections, but each time the feds bailed him out because, as a DEA agent said, "They didn't want to lose him. He beat the system because he had the contacts to smuggle large quantities of dope for us. That means drug seizure statistics, promotions, and careers."

An investigative report released by the U.S. House Committee on Government Operation in August 1992 revealed that in the prior two years, the Justice Department alone had spent $28.6 million paying informants, 65 of whom were paid more than $100,000 each, 24 of whom were paid between $100,000 and $250,000, and 8 of whom got more than $250,000. The FBI paid out $11 million in the same period.

In the case involving the murder of a DEA agent, Enrique Camarena, by Mexican nationals, which has yet to go to trial, the government has already paid out $2.7 million to informants. One of these informants is Rene Lopez-Romero, allegedly involved in the 1984 kidnapping and murder of four American missionaries in Guadalajara, Mexico, who is being paid $3,000 monthly until the trial. Another informant in the case has received $909,862 stemming from still another forfeiture case in which he provided information.

SECRET PAY FOR A HELL'S ANGEL

Much of the federal informant program is shrouded in deep secrecy, not just to protect the identity of the informers from prospective targets of their clandestine activity, but also because of the highly unsavory nature of the informers themselves. For example, Anthony Tait, a former member of the Hell's Angels motorcycle gang and admitted drug addict, earned nearly $1 million between 1985 and 1988 as a federal informer according to a copy of his payment schedule and his FBI contract obtained by the *Pittsburgh Press*. These payments included $250,000 as a share of assets forfeited as a result of his cooperation, with payments coming from FBI offices in Anchorage and San Francisco, $40,000 in salary and expenses from the DEA, and payments from the California and federal asset forfeiture funds.

The public got a rare glimpse of what goes on when Edward Vaughn testified in court that he had run a multimillion dollar international drug smuggling ring, been a federal fugitive, and twice served time in prison before arranging early release as a result of agreeing to work as a paid informant for the federal government. Vaughn was paid a $40,000 annual salary and expenses by the DEA and $500 monthly by the U.S. Marshals Service. His contract called for payment of 25 percent of all assets he caused to be forfeited to the federal government. The *Pittsburgh Press* reported, "Vaughn said he preferred arranging deals . . . known as 'reverse stings;' the law enforcement agents pose as drug sellers and the targets bring cash for the buys. Those deals take cash, but not drugs, off the street. In those stings, he said, cash would be forfeited and Vaughn would get his prearranged quarter share."

BIG CITY BLUNDERS

And when some police don't have a reliable informant on which to base a "probable cause" request for a search or arrest warrant, they invent them.

Boston

A 1988 investigation of the Boston Police Drug Control Unit revealed that its police members routinely fabricated the existence of informants and lied to obtain warrants from judges. At 3:15 on the afternoon of March 26, 1994, a 13-member SWAT team from this same police unit, wearing helmets, fatigues, and boots and armed with shotguns and 9mm Glock pistols, sledgehammered through the apartment door of a 75-year-old black minister, Rev. Acelynne Williams. They were searching for guns and drugs (never found) based on a statement of yet another "confidential informant." At 3:58 P.M., Rev. Williams (5 feet 7 and 1/2 inches tall, 155 pounds) was pronounced dead of a heart attack after being forced to the floor and handcuffed by three police officers, two holding his arms, one pinning his legs. Once he was "secure," the police noticed he was vomiting and breathing heavily and called an ambulance. The autopsy showed he died of acute myocardial infarction brought on by heart disease and "emotional stress." Six weeks and two official investigations later, the Boston police commissioner concluded the police had mistakenly raided the wrong apartment, partly because of a bad tip from their informant, who had been drunk the night he visited the alleged den of guns and drugs, partly because of bad police work and because of lack of proper supervision and regulations governing the use of confidential informers. Four police officers were reassigned to other jobs, and six had disciplinary charges lodged against them. It turned out that the informant (name unknown) in the case, aside from having an alcohol-impaired memory, had been arrested two years before for firing a gun at several police officers. In court arguments the government stated that his tips were usually "considered reliable."

New York

Apparently, lying by police to support criminal charges is common—certainly so in New York City, according to a draft report of the mayor's commission investigating police corruption. After months of hearings in 1993 and 1994, the commission concluded that New York police often make false arrests, tamper with evidence, and commit perjury on the witness stand. "Perjury is the most widespread form of police wrongdoing," the report stated, noting it even has a well-known nickname among the courthouse cognoscente—"testilying." According to New York Legal Aid Society officials, "testilying" is a common police practice that goes on without sanction by prosecutors or judges, who often cooperate by not challenging the officers' tailoring of testimony to meet constitutional objections or deficiencies in police work or reports.

At the same time this draft report was released, 14 officers were arrested in New York's 30th precinct in central Harlem, charged with scores of shakedowns of drug dealers, assaults, accepting of bribes for protection, stealing of drugs and cash from dealers, and selling of confiscated drugs themselves. Millions of dollars worth of cash and drugs were involved in these charges, much of it confiscated in forfeitures. Many more police were rumored to be slated for arrest.

Cleveland

The following is one last example of the unquestioned "reliability" of informers. In the summer of 1992 in Cleveland, Ohio, two inspectors of the U.S. Postal Service arrested 19 postal workers and a local community activist, all accused of dealing drugs based on the undercover work of two paid informants who were allowed to pose as postal workers. When the first case went to trial in state court it immediately fell apart. The informers had faked the tape recordings of the accused dealing drugs; the voice was not even his. It turned out the two informers had bilked the Postal Service out of $250,000 in postal funds they were supposed to use in setting up drug deals and making purchases. Instead, they pocketed the money and gave the postal inspectors bags of baking soda laced with a little cocaine. Five similar Postal Service cases also came to light in other parts of the country where informers had similarly duped the Service. Most of the 19 falsely accused Ohio postal workers were dismissed, some lost their homes, several divorced, and one attempted suicide before the informer fraud was discovered.

COUNTRY SNITCHES

Perhaps you have a desire to invest in farmland, to acquire a few bucolic acres at a bargain price—back to nature, so to speak. Maybe you should think again.

Not all police departments have available the bloated resources of the federal government; in many rural areas local police must depend on cut-rate informants who too often prove the truth of that old adage, "You get what you pay for."

A case in point is a man whose name is Mudd—Steve R.

Mudd. Starting in November 1989, Mudd was the one and only undercover agent (paid $4.65 an hour, barely minimum wage) in a marijuana investigation near Kirksville, Missouri, in rural Adair County in the northwest corner of the state. Mudd had been in drug rehabilitation, convicted of possession and sale of drugs, and had a history of writing bad checks. He was always broke and had no visible means of support other than odd jobs and his police pay for Operation BAD ("Bust a Dealer"). In the course of his year's "work," Mudd's "eyewitness information" was used to arrest 35 people. These included Matthew Farrell, a farmer Mudd accused of selling and cultivating pot on his 60-acre farm in an elaborate story that described night harvesting of pot with specially equipped tractors. The sheriff arrested Farrell and ordered his house and farm seized for forfeiture. As you may have guessed, a meticulous search with vacuum cleaners failed to turn up even one marijuana seed on the Farrell farm, in the house, or anywhere else. All 35 state drug cases based on Mudd's statements, including Farrell's, "went down the tubes," as county prosecutor Tom Hensley described it.

But under Missouri law, proceeds from civil asset forfeitures must go directly into the state's general fund for school programs, not to the police. Knowing this, Hensley took advantage of a federal law that permits a state or local agency to convert a state seizure into a federal forfeiture. When feds "adopt" the state seizure as their own, which they routinely do upon request, the state or local agency is eligible for up to 85 percent of the net proceeds from the forfeiture. And even in rural Adair County, a 60-acre farm is worth something, even if no pot is being grown there. Said attorney Hensley, "The federal sharing plan is what affected how the case was brought. . . . Seizures are kind of like bounties anyway, so why shouldn't I take it to the feds so the money comes back to the local law enforcement effort?"

And what happened to Farrell and his farm? When last heard from, he and his wife were tied up in a federal forfeiture proceeding in U.S. District Court in St. Louis, notwithstanding the fact that all state criminal charges had been dismissed against him personally. County prosecutor Hensley said he didn't think Mudd had "scammed us that bad . . . there is marijuana use here, and we had to get somebody. We don't get big enough cases here to get the state police here to do an investigation up right." Asked why he did not seek to have the forfeiture case dropped by federal authorities, Hensley said he was not inclined "to call down to St. Louis and tell the U.S. Attorney to drop it. I've got other things to do with my time. I don't want to sound malicious, but this will all work out." Assistant U.S. Attorney Daniel Meuleman acknowledged that any federal case would be based on the same facts as the original state case, "but that doesn't mean we can't go ahead because there are different standards of proof involved"—meaning "beyond reasonable doubt"—to convict farmer Farrell on drug charges in state court, but only "probable cause" to take away his farm in federal court. Mr. Meuleman refused to say whether he would call Mudd as a witness.

Is it any wonder Americans are cynical about government?

CHAPTER

5

The U.S. Supreme Court Finally Acts

In a series of cases decided in 1993, the U.S. Supreme Court at long last established important and much needed constitutional limitations on criminal and civil forfeiture. Until then, most federal courts seemed willing to allow unlimited expansion of government forfeiture powers.

There was little reason lower courts should have done otherwise. Just 20 years ago, the Supreme Court itself reaffirmed the triumph of mindless government forfeiture over the rights of an innocent property owner. Its holding was based solely on forfeiture's historical family tree, with little consideration of logic, equity, or the practical needs of a modern society. In that 1974 case, *Caldero-Toledo v. Pearson Yacht Leasing Co.*, 416 U.S. 663, (which government attorneys subsequently cited endlessly as authority for every and any forfeiture action), a yacht leasing company gave a charter

for one of its ships for a trip from Florida to Puerto Rico. The charter document specified no illegal conduct was to occur aboard the
ship. Government agents later found one marijuana joint, possibly
left by someone who was aboard during the charter, and confiscated
the ship, valued at hundreds of thousands of dollars. The Supreme
Court said the leasing company had not done "all that it reasonably
could to avoid having its property put to an unlawful use," but the
Court never said what the company could or should have done.
(Perhaps go along as an uninvited nautical nanny?) As justification
for its surrealistic decision (holding the yacht itself guilty for the pot
found aboard), the Court simply recited a superbly researched history of forfeiture dating back to the English kings. In effect it said,
"That's the way this legal fiction has always operated; that's the way
it still works now." The *Caldero-Toledo* decision became a wholesale
license for law enforcement officers to do as they pleased with forfeitures and, worst of all, placed a ridiculous legal fiction and its
associated history above the hard-won provisions of the American
Bill of Rights.

BUENA VISTA AVENUE—THE "TAINT" DOCTRINE

With this strange legal history and its fairy-tale characteristics
as a backdrop, on February 24, 1993, in *United States v. Buena Vista
Avenue, Rumson, New Jersey*, 113 S.Ct. 1126, the Supreme Court
seriously curtailed any further expansion of one major facet of these
pro-government legal fictions known as the "relation back" doctrine. In essence, this theory held that at the very moment in time
at which an illegal act punishable by forfeiture occurs on a piece of
real estate, that crime "taints" the land or building and immediately, automatically "vests" in the government all right, title, and interest to the property. Magic? Well, in this quaint hypothesis we do
hear a faint echo of the English common law and the medieval "evil
taint" cast upon an offending object.

In *Buena Vista* the Justice Department unsuccessfully argued,
relying on the taint doctrine, that because subsequent "owners"
were blocked from receiving a good title because of the taint, they
were not "innocent owners" entitled to raise that status as a defense

to forfeiture. The Court disagreed, saying that until a court renders judgment in a forfeiture case, any prior owner of the property at issue has a good title—and the right to defend that title as an innocent owner or with any other applicable defense.

AUSTIN—PROPORTIONALITY

A second judicial blow to police forfeiture power came on June 28, 1993, in *Austin v. United States*, 113 S.Ct. 2801, an *in rem* civil proceeding in which the Supreme Court, in a rare unanimous opinion, held first that civil forfeitures are subject to the limits of the Eighth Amendment, which forbids excessive fines and cruel and unusual punishments, and second, that forfeitures cannot be excessive in relation to the offense committed. The issue arose after Richard Austin's guilty plea to a South Dakota state drug charge of selling two ounces of cocaine, worth about $2,000, for which he received a sentence of eight years in prison. Subsequently, the government moved to forfeit Austin's home and auto body shop, a punishment the Court held was disproportionate to his crime. The Court did not set out an exact test for proportionality, leaving that for development by lower federal courts—which means it will be years before we know what the exact parameters of the test will turn out to be.

Perhaps the most significant aspect of the Court's *Austin* ruling was its rejection, for the first time, of the government's traditional argument that civil forfeitures are not "punitive," but rather "remedial." Most lower courts routinely accepted the government's argument that forfeitures were simply "remedial" in nature, that to seize property, regardless of its value, was to remove the tools of criminal conduct and reimburse the government for the costs of law enforcement. It was this venerable legal fiction that for a century allowed courts to exempt forfeiture cases from normal due process requirements imposed by the Fifth Amendment, which do apply in all cases where a person (as compared to property) is accused of a crime. By holding that the civil forfeiture provision of the drug statute was in fact "punishment," the Court opened the door to challenges asking that due process guarantees, such as the presumption of innocence and proof beyond a reasonable doubt, be applied to forfeiture cases. Again, only time will tell how far the Court will go, but at least this new due process trend is in the right direction.

ALEXANDER—THE EIGHTH AMENDMENT LIVES

In a companion case handed down the same day as *Austin*, involving racketeering, obscenity, and criminal forfeiture brought under the RICO statute, *Alexander v. United States*, 113 S.Ct. 2766, the Court decided that the government's taking of $9 million in business profits and $25 million in business assets (including 10 pieces of real estate—and more than 100,000 books and video-tapes, which the government summarily destroyed) from Ferris J. Alexander also may have been disproportionate and excessive under the Eighth Amendment. Alexander had been convicted of selling 11 obscene books and videotapes. The case was remanded for lower court determination of the proportionality issue. Alexander had already been fined $100,000 and sentenced to six years imprisonment.

The Court rejected, 5-4, Alexander's First Amendment "free-dom of expression" claims. Every American should be disturbed by the wider implications of this aspect of the case, which are truly chilling for American freedom. Based on this theory, police could seize a few books or videotapes claiming them to be "obscene" from one store operated by, say, Blockbuster Video or Brentano's, B. Dalton, Barnes & Noble, Crown Books, or any chain of similar retailers. Police could then close down all the stores in the chain and destroy the contents of every store, all without a trial and before any judicial consideration of the merits of these acts. What does such official conduct amount to, if not book burning?

In his dissent in *Alexander*, Justice Anthony Kennedy com-mented as follows: "Until now I thought one could browse through any book or film store in the United States without fear that the proprietor had chosen each item to avoid risk to his inventory and indeed to the business itself. . . . This ominous, onerous threat undermines free speech and press principles essen-tial to our freedom."

No More Double Jeopardy

There had been a few hints that the Supreme Court was moving in this new direction on forfeiture before the 1993 rulings. One came in *United States v. Halper*, 490 U.S. 435 (1989), in which the Court held that civil forfeiture actions following a criminal conviction (in this instance of a doctor who had overbilled the government $585) may be so severe as to constitute an unconstitutional second criminal punishment for the same offense. In a civil action the government sought to obtain $130,000 in "remedial penalties" from Dr. Halper under the False Claims Act, in addition to his criminal punishment of a fine of $5,000 and two years imprisonment. The Court said such punishment "bore no rational relationship to the goal of compensating the government for its loss" and that the action, which they held to be punitive in nature, was therefore barred by the double jeopardy clause of the Fifth Amendment to the Constitution.

GOOD AFFIRMS DUE PROCESS

On December 13, 1993, the Supreme Court capped a year of forfeiture reform, deciding yet another case which can be called a victory on this issue. In *United States v. James Daniel Good Real Property*, 114 S.Ct. 492, the Court held that the due process clause requires that before an owner can be deprived of his or her real property—whether it be his home or any other real property—he is entitled to notice and a hearing. (The decision did not include personal property, autos, cash, bank accounts, or corporate or other businesses.) Before the *Good* decision, without the property owner's knowing it, and without a hearing, the government could obtain a seizure warrant based on hearsay or a secret informer's statements and evict the owner the same day.

POLICE OPPOSITION TO CHANGE

In spite of these hopeful Supreme Court decisions, there is not going to be a big change overnight. These cases now must be applied in lower federal courts, and it will take years to know their full

impact. Meanwhile, they do offer a little increased property protection and the possibility of due process procedural changes. It is
important to bear in mind that the Supreme Court will frequently
reverse a well-publicized case that has drawn excessive media attention but draw its decision in such narrow terms that it is meaning-
less as a precedent and only applies to the particular case. Other
seizures continue as normal, but many gullible members of the public believe that the Court has ordered some particular practice
stopped because a newspaper headline or television story says that
the Court reversed a particular case. Other times the Supreme Court
returns a case to the lower court to reconsider a particular issue,
which again does not mean that anything significant happened, yet
most people believe that the Supreme Court has made some major
decision that stops the practice.

But the police are not about to stop forfeiture activity, which
continues without pause.

Police all across this nation have intimate daily knowledge of
tragic events such as those you have read about here. Knowing what
is going on, you might think reasonable law enforcement officials at
all levels of government would be in the vanguard, asking for reasonable reforms in civil asset forfeiture law—not just to protect
innocent citizens and their property rights, but to protect the police
themselves from the stigma of operating like a gang of professional
thieves with official immunity from prosecution.

Perhaps the lure of millions of dollars for police salaries, equipment, and technical advances is too great to overcome. But too
often the crass police attitude is that expressed by Sheriff Bob Vogel
of Volusia County, Florida: "If you don't like the statutes . . . then
you get the doggone statutes changed. We don't have to prove the
fact they [property owners] are guilty."

Indeed, if you listen to the police and prosecutorial rhetoric
loosed in response to proposed forfeiture reform, you would think
the end of the world is at hand. Even moderate forfeiture reforms
have been officially opposed by the Department of Justice, the
National Association of Attorneys General, and the National
District Attorneys Association. In 1991 when the Uniform Law
Commission (the national conference seeking to harmonize state

laws by drafting model statutes) suggested mild forfeiture reforms, all three of the above-named parties took the unprecedented step of formally withdrawing as participants in the Commission's deliberations as a protest. Instead, they presented their own "Model Asset Forfeiture Act," which contains no reforms of current law but gives government massive new powers to take property by forfeiture. These government "special interests" benefit from close to three quarters of a billion dollars a year from forfeitures at the federal and state levels, and they are not about to let go of the golden egg-laying goose.

On the federal level, a typical negative official attitude toward forfeiture reform was arrogantly displayed by Lee J. Radek, director of the Department of Justice's Asset Forfeiture Office. In a 1993 statement (and therefore, we can assume it represents official Clinton administration policy), Radek reviewed the U.S. Supreme Court decisions in the *Buena Vista* and *Austin* cases, acknowledging "the problems" these affirmations of property owners' rights would cause the federal forfeiture program. Apparently oblivious to the fundamental constitutional issues raised in those important cases, or the Article III role of constitutional interpretation assigned to the nation's highest court in our social and political system, Radek described the decisions as "a pretty good beating from the Supreme Court," then went on to predict that Congress might adopt forfeiture reform "with dubious results probable." He then lumped the Supreme Court and Congress together with "the enemies of forfeiture," all of who delight in "kicking a good program when it's down . . . increasing the intensity of their attacks." Radek impudently predicted he and his associates would come up with new methods of "innovative expansion" to get around the Supreme Court.

Small wonder that bipartisan congressional efforts to pass a forfeiture reform bill have met with Justice Department stonewalling.

Modern Despots
Like the British Crown agents in colonial America, their modern American police counterparts are dependent on an unjust confiscatory system to pay their way. Today's confiscators differ little in

attitude or action from their royal predecessors. The irony is that the latest users of the coercive forfeiture power, supposed heirs of the American Revolution against a despot who used it to fleece our ancestors, now employ the same tyrannical weapon.

The true motive behind forfeitures is greed, often both personal and official. Current forfeiture law allows too great a temptation for mere mortals to resist. Armed with legal impunity, government officials take private citizens' property, sell it, keep the proceeds, and create for themselves a limitless budget without oversight by anyone. Police can pick items of real and personal property for their "official" use as they please—and so private country clubs become police training schools, district attorneys drive new BMWs, and luxury acquisitions, which elected officials would never approve, abound as fancy supplements to police budgets from coast to coast.

Is it any wonder that along with rape squads and murder details, we now have official police "forfeiture squads" out scouring the town in order to meet quotas, not for arrests and convictions, but for total dollar value confiscated? This "new math" dictates that a policeman can aim at a $1 million residence—rather than a mere $100 in the pocket of a street-level drug dealer. Besides, real criminals pose real risks. They have guns, and they can be violent. Innocent property owners can't resist forfeiture, unless they can afford to pay lawyers thousands of dollars—and even then the outcome is in doubt for years.

How to Protect
Your Own Assets

The information, events, data, and case histories described here concerning government forfeiture are all true. As bizarre as some of these stories seem, the same or similar things could happen to you. You don't have to be paranoid to realize how vulnerable your real estate or other property is to police confiscation. Now that you know, use this valuable information to make safe investments and as a guide for conduct in your business and personal life. Also consider that police and their legislative friends in Congress and the states are always trying to pass new and tougher forfeiture laws. Keep abreast of these changes in the law and act accordingly.

Of course, the only real way to avoid civil asset forfeiture is to own no real property in America. That's sounds drastic, but it is true. If you are thinking of buying real estate, think again. And if you are already a property owner, maybe you should consider selling.

Americans have always cherished their right to "life, liberty, and the pursuit of happiness." Now you know that for many citizens who own property, all three of those objectives are in serious doubt. Now that you are forewarned, be sure to take every reasonable precaution to make certain it's not you—or your property that's being pursued. The chapters that follow offer some advice on how to best accomplish that.

CHAPTER 6

What to Avoid and Beware Of

As you read Part I of this book, considering the problems asset forfeiture presents an investor, no doubt you were also thinking about ways personally to avoid this horrible possibility.

Be careful. The familiar "tried and true" asset protection devices we all know don't always work in forfeiture cases—and their use may well make things worse if the government confiscates your property.

This creates a major dilemma: the very things that you should do to protect yourself against lawsuits won't protect you against the government itself. Although most readers will be quite content with normal asset protection devices and will primarily fear ordinary lawsuits, you should consider carefully what degree of protection you are seeking and whom you want to be protected from.

If you decide that you are as concerned about the government as private litigants, then you should instruct your asset protection professional to use primarily offshore vehicles that will keep your property outside of the jurisdiction of the U.S. government. We will take a look at some of those options later on, but first, let's look at some things that can be considered financial faux pas when it comes to protecting yourself against government forfeiture. We'll also look at some situations you may not have considered that may make you, as an investor, an unwitting participant in criminal activity and therefore vulnerable to forfeiture.

SOME ASSET PROTECTION
DEVICES THAT FALL SHORT

If, as an antiforfeiture device, you are thinking about putting title to property in the name of "straw owners," third parties, partnerships, corporations, or trusts, think again. All of these devices have been tested in various state and federal courts in forfeiture cases—and all have been found wanting. While all of them make it more difficult for others to locate your assets, and some have distinct tax or avoidance of probate advantages, they also lessen your control and make it difficult to liquidate in an emergency such as threatened forfeiture. Worst of all, many courts in forfeiture proceedings view these devices as additional evidence of, or possible attempts to conceal, the criminal activity in which the police allege the property is involved.

Straw Ownership

All of the reasons against putting your assets in someone else's name apply to forfeiture as well: the property becomes susceptible to the straw owner's debts, bankruptcy, and criminal acts. And spouses, children, and best friends do have a way of changing dramatically over time.

Also, in a number of court cases the straw title holder has been refused the right to defend against forfeiture based on the government's contention that the owner of record is in fact not the true and beneficial owner.

Corporations

Family corporations, especially those created to hold title to real estate, are often recommended as an asset protection method. Unfortunately, they are of little use against forfeiture actions. If you are fighting government lawyers over a valuable parcel of real estate, you can bet the feds will make sure that from its inception your "corporation" has met every requirement of law—annual meetings, minutes, stock issues, notice, and election of officers and directors. Otherwise, you can expect to witness the actual event that most lawyers only study in law school—"piercing the corporate veil." That means your corporate structure will do you no good as a defense against confiscation of corporate real estate for alleged criminal acts. Some federal courts have even held the act of incorporation to hold title to real property is evidence of planned "concealment," and therefore a basis for probable cause supporting forfeiture.

Family Partnerships

Terri Todd-Brown learned the hard way that a family partnership doesn't work against forfeiture. She and her two sisters each held 33 percent of the equal shares of a family winery partnership, while her father, as managing partner, held 1 percent. To avoid probate, the agreement allowed Dad to live on the Tennessee farm for life and manage the winery, although the sisters took an active interest in its business affairs for years, contributing "sweat equity." Unbeknownst to the girls, Dad was growing marijuana along with the grapes. After the feds confiscated the farm (Dad was found dead "of a heart attack" during the raid), a Tennessee court held that for the purposes of defending against forfeiture the sisters had no standing since it was a sham partnership and they were never true owners (this in spite of the family partnership having met all requirements of Tennessee law and the Uniform Partnership Act!).

Family Trusts

You can bet the government has many ways to find out who the beneficial owners of a land trust are, and anyway, to the forfeiture brigades, it does not matter. They can and do treat a trust as a sham, and a trust will not deter their power to seize the property.

Besides, it costs plenty to establish and maintain a trust, and federal courts have even held that the beneficiaries of a trust have no standing to defend trust assets against civil forfeiture. And trustees can be pressured.

Fellow Investors

Be very careful about fellow investors with whom you combine your money or assets, especially when purchasing real estate. Alleged profits from any number of crimes, if used even as a small part of the payment for real estate, subjects the property to confiscation. Under the current Justice Department theory, $1 of "tainted" money subjects an entire bank account—or anything the account is used to buy—to forfeiture. The money-laundering statute allows forfeiture of "any property, real or personal, involved in a transaction or attempted transaction." Remember, all the government has to do is allege the money is tainted; you have to prove it isn't! So check out your fellow investors with great care. And keep in mind the more successful a money laundering operation is the more difficult it is for you to find that out.

Failure to Report Money Transactions

Another thing to consider carefully is that failure to report cash transactions (including importing capital from abroad) in amounts of $10,000 or more to the IRS means anything the money buys is open to forfeiture. In 1990 the U.S. Treasury established a new super computer system (called "FinCEN") in Arlington, Virginia, near Washington, D.C., to allow all federal and state police agencies to obtain information and cross-check all financial transactions for possible criminal prosecution and forfeiture. Any corporation or individual can be subjected to such a check, and thousands already have.

GUILTY BY ASSOCIATION

Under forfeiture your property can be confiscated based on any criminal act that occurs on the premises.

As a homeowner, therefore, you must keep a careful watch on

your children, relatives, and guests. Pot smoking in private or drug use at a party—even if you don't know about it—can put your home in jeopardy. When police respond to a neighbor's complaint about excessive noise and smell pot in the air, your house may go up in smoke too.

In 1991 Gussie Mae Gantt of Montgomery, Alabama, an elderly widow, discovered her adult children were selling drugs out of her home. She evicted them, put up "No Trespassing" signs to ward off street dealers, and repeatedly called the police to report drug activity near her house. Police made no arrests but six months later obtained a warrant and searched her house, finding no evidence of drugs. Nevertheless, a federal magistrate ordered Ms. Gantt's home seized based on police affidavits. U.S. Attorney Jim Wilson, in trying to justify the forfeiture, accused Ms. Gantt of complicity in drug crimes, saying, "Anybody that owns property can do more than [she did] to keep crack dealers from selling drugs." A U.S. district judge wasn't buying Wilson's line; he ordered her house returned, saying, she "took all reasonable steps a person of her abilities could be expected to take." The judge also ordered the Justice Department to pay all her legal expenses—but later reversed himself on this point at Justice Department urging, agreeing that "probable cause" had existed for the government's forfeiture initiation.

Rental Properties

You can lose your apartment house or duplex if your tenants are engaged in criminal conduct. If you think they are, consider eviction, or at least make inquiries and document your discovery efforts in writing. Reporting your suspicions to the police is a two-edged sword: if you don't, your failure could implicate you in concealing a crime; if you do and the activity is allowed to continue, you still may be held responsible. Make sure leases clearly forbid criminal conduct. Make sure vacant property or units are fully secured so they cannot be used for illegal purposes. On this point, you should obviously avoid investing in property located in "slum" areas where there is a much greater chance of its illegal use—even if the potential profit may be greater. Remember, the whole tract of land can be taken for illegal conduct that occurs on any part of the land. Drug sales in a parking lot can mean the loss of the entire apartment building.

The problem faced by landlords was highlighted in the forfeiture of a three-unit rental building in Englewood, California, owned
by a retired army officer and his wife. As a result of drug activity in
the building, the police confiscated the apartment house without
notice to the owners, who had been reluctant to act on their own
without proof or police assistance. The 9th Circuit U.S. Court of
Appeals upheld the seizure, saying the owners were guilty of "willful
dereliction of social responsibility." When asked for comment, Los
Angeles police officer Carlos Lopez said, "We're trying to have owners take responsibility for the people they rent to. . . . It's part of
being an owner."

Admittedly, there is a civic duty to report criminal conduct,
but private citizens, even if they are owners of rental properties,
should not be forced to do the job of policemen. Without any means
of physical self-defense, no power of arrest, no right to search private
rental units, and no immunity from civil suit based on invasion of
privacy or slander, how can a landlord reasonably be required to
"take responsibility for the people they rent to," as Officer Lopez and
the 9th Circuit would have it? Indeed, this expanding concept of
owner responsibility for tenants' activities is an easy way for government, failing in the war on drugs, to shift blame for its dereliction to private citizens.

Condos

One of the advantages of having a condo are the tax breaks
that depend on your renting the condo during most of the year.
Renting means tenants and their guests, and condos are usually used
for vacations. Vacations mean drugs to many people. You can easily
see what may happen to your favorite ski place at Vail or your
beachfront unit on South Padre Island unless you rent with great
care. And don't forget to impress on the management agency you
hire for your condo or apartments the need to be vigilant about possible criminal activity on your property.

Commercial Property

Hotels, motels, bars, and restaurants that are likely to attract a
fast crowd and drug transactions are to be avoided at all costs as

investments. Avoid underworld types, don't ignore police warnings about possible criminal conduct on your premises, and keep a watchful eye.

Jesse Bunch owned a bar and residential apartments in a highly active drug trafficking area in upstate New York. He did know of drug selling activity on his premises but took many steps to prevent it. He fired two bartenders after they were arrested at the bar for drug violations, evicted two residents following their arrests, restricted use of the rest rooms, posted signs advising patrons that they were subject to search and seizure, restricted the bar's hours of operations, and periodically called police to report drug activity in the vicinity of his property. However, drug activity continued, and, Bunch's valiant efforts notwithstanding, the government seized the property.

Luckily for Mr. Bunch, although the government argued against him, an appellate court ruled that he was protected by the innocent-owner defense because of his lack of consent to the illegal drug trafficking and his reasonable efforts to end it. "Mr. Bunch, who was trying to eke out an income from a business located in a drug-infested area that posed great risks to the safety of him and his family . . . fulfilled his legal obligation," said the court.

Farm Land and Undeveloped Property

One assistant United States attorney argued in a forfeiture case before a federal court of appeals that the Justice Department had the power to "seize the King Ranch, the legendary Texas spread covering hundreds of square miles, were we to detect an illegal crap game in one stable."

Tracts of land in rural areas—the larger and more remote parcels in particular—are favorite places for clandestine cultivation of marijuana, often unbeknownst to the land owners. It is estimated that from 1 to 3 million Americans grow pot, from 100,000 to 200,000 of them for commercial sale—especially in a nine-state region of the Midwest where growing conditions are best. Plants are placed in between rows of corn or among trees that conceal them from aerial observation by police. In 1992 340,000 Americans were arrested for pot violations, a quarter of them for cultivation and sale. Plausible estimates of the cash value of America's annual crop of marijuana range from $4 billion to $24 billion. (The value of America's largest legal cash crop, corn, was $16 billion in 1993.) What all these numbers mean is that a farm owner's welfare is not a major concern of pot growers. But the owner is the one who suffers forfeiture. Inspect your corn rows.

For example, local police found five hundred marijuana plants growing on a retiree's 37-acre farm in Kentucky. Delmar Puryear, who had retired with a disability and could not farm, insisted that he knew nothing about the plants. Marijuana grows wild all over the Midwestern states, a by-product of the massive illegal cultivation that thrives there today. A jury apparently believed Mr. Puryear, finding him innocent of state criminal charges. Despite this acquittal, the federal government refused to drop its efforts to seize the farm until Puryear agreed to pay $12,500 to reimburse the government for its legal costs.

Office Buildings

In April 1988 the On Leong Chinese Merchants Association building in Chicago, a three-story landmark in the city's Chinatown, was seized by the feds for alleged gambling activity, which they said had occurred on three occasions between 1984 and 1986. The federal court not only refused to allow the Chinese Merchants to have discovery of government documents so they could defend their case, it granted summary judgment to the government, allowing forfeiture without a trial!

You might want to consider this case and the language of the federal antigambling statute (18 U.S.C. sec. 1955) when next you are asked to permit an office football pool in your building. That law says owners of buildings in which illegal gambling takes place will have the property forfeited unless they can prove by a preponderance of the evidence they were uninvolved in and unaware of the illegal use of their property—and that they did everything they reasonably could be expected to do to prevent it.

Would the feds confiscate an office building because of a football pool? Ask the On Leong Chinese Merchants what they think.

On March 4, 1996, the U.S. Supreme Court upheld Michigan's forfeiture of a wife's interest in a car that her husband used, without her knowledge, to pick up a prostitute. The Court held as follows: "Her claim that she was entitled to contest the abatement by showing that she did not know that her husband would use the car to violate state law is defeated by a long and unbroken line of cases in which this Court has held that an owner's interest in property may be forfeited by reason of the use to which the property is put even though the owner did not know that it was to be put to such use."

SOME INVESTOR TIPS ABOUT FORFEITURE

Don't Buy Forfeited Property. Every Sunday the business section of the *New York Times* contains a full-page ad purchased by the U.S. government listing real and personal property forfeitures from all over the country. *USA Today* has a similar full-page listing each week. Any property police confiscate but don't wish to keep for their own use is sold to raise cash for "law enforcement." That's why you read and hear about "police sales," at which you supposedly can obtain great bargains.

Don't even consider making a purchase at such a government sale. Aside from the fact that you would probably be buying stolen property (stolen by the government), a good and clear title to forfeited property is very difficult to obtain, and title insurance is virtually impossible to buy. Boats or motor vehicles are usually thoroughly trashed by the time the police dump them on the auction block. Homes or other buildings receive little or no care or maintenance once the government grabs them, and a purchaser buys all the troubles that such neglect produces. In almost every case, forfeited property is reduced to a fraction of its former value because of government vandalism—a fact supported by no less than nine official studies of forfeited property issued by the U.S. Government Accounting Office, the independent investigative arm of Congress.

Be Wary of Seller Financing. Be extremely selective about whom you sell your home or other real property to if you intend to take back a mortgage to finance the sale. Numerous federal court cases brought by banks and finance companies have held that a mortgage lien holder is powerless to foreclose on property once the government seizes it. This means that if your purchaser turns out to be a drug dealer or pornographer or is indicted for alleged RICO crimes, as in one California case, it could require a decade or more for the courts to determine your rights to the property, and then you may get nothing but a worthless wrecked building (assuming you win the case at all, that is).

Practice Effective Leasing. If you are a landlord, make sure your lawyer drafts an "eviction for cause" clause in all leases allowing you to remove tenants if they engage in conduct which might cause government confiscation. Landlord-tenant laws vary widely from state to state, but most favor the tenant. Don't base the eviction clause on "criminal conduct," which would be nearly impossible for you to prove. Make eviction contingent on events such as allowing people to loiter on the premises after a warning from you, or on excessive numbers of people coming and going from the rental property or unit. If your rentals are commercial, make eviction contingent on illegal sales of such things as drug paraphernalia or other described illegal conduct.

Use Law-Abiding Rental Managers. Make sure your rental property management company or your manager has a clean record and is not engaging in any illegal conduct on the premises or allowing such conduct. Property managers who allow drug activity or other illegal conduct are a major reason for police confiscation.

Guard Your Paper Trail. Never create a document, including a diary, which you don't want to have used against you in court, especially as it pertains to your property. Let your attorneys keep records for you. That gives them the legal protection of the attorney-client privilege. Do document your efforts to check the good character of tenants before you rent to them or other efforts you make to assure your property is used in a legal manner. And be very careful about where you discard papers or records. It is standard practice for cops to go through your trash seeking evidence on which to base property forfeiture.

7

International Asset Protection Trusts

Recently the international asset protection trust (APT) has gained popularity. This foreign trust often appears to be attractive to persons wishing to shield personal assets from possible forfeiture or other potential liability.

PROTECTION AGAINST THE UNEXPECTED

Medical, legal, and professional malpractice suits, as well as legislative and judicial imposition of no-fault personal liability on corporate officers and directors, have by now become a fact of U.S. business life. An active business or professional person can suddenly be held responsible for all sorts of unforeseen events, such as a company's environmental pollution, a bank failure, or a dissatisfied client. Premiums for malpractice insurance have gone through the roof. In this business climate, astute people must consider the best way to protect their personal assets against any eventuality.

One way to place those assets beyond the reach of potential litigation plaintiffs, creditors, and their contingent-fee lawyers is through the creation of an asset protection trust located in a foreign country where the law favors such goals. Certain of these foreign jurisdictions do not recognize U.S. or any nondomestic court orders, and a creditor must retry completely the original claim which gave rise to the U.S. judgment.

The country chosen for such a trust must have local trust experts who understand fully and are able to assist you in your objectives. The foreign local attorney who creates your trust unquestionably must know the applicable law and tax consequences, or you will be in trouble from the start.

Once established, the offshore asset protection trust in its basic form can consist of as little as a trust account in an international bank located in the foreign country. Many well established multinational banks can provide trustees for such arrangements and are experienced in such matters. With today's instant communications and international banking facilities, it is as convenient to hold assets and accounts overseas as it is in another American city. Most international banks offer U.S. dollar-denominated accounts that often offer better interest rates than U.S. institutions.

PROS AND CONS

Depending on the country of choice, the settlor of a foreign asset protection trust can gain many advantages, including the exercise of far greater control over assets and income from the trust than permitted under U.S. domestic law. Generally, the U.S. rule that does not permit a settlor to create a trust for his own benefit does not apply in foreign countries. Creation of such a trust also means removal of your assets as a lawsuit target, since domestic creditors are discouraged when faced with enforcement of a U.S. judgment in another country. However, the greater degree of control over the assets that the settlor maintains, the easier it is for a U.S. court, which has jurisdiction over the settlor, to order the settlor to return the assets to the jurisdiction of the court.

The trust can provide privacy, confidentiality, and reduced domestic reporting requirements in your own country; avoidance of domestic taxes and probate in case of death; and increased flexibility in conducting affairs in case of disability, in transferring assets, in investing internationally, or in avoiding domestic currency controls. A foreign asset protection trust can also substitute for or supplement costly professional liability insurance or even a prenuptial agreement as protection for your heirs and their inheritance.

TRUST CREATION ABROAD

The structure of foreign asset protection trusts is not very different from that of an American trust. The settlor creates the trust and transfers the title to his assets to the trust to be administered according to the trust declaration by the trustees. Usually the trustee is a bank in the jurisdiction chosen. Beneficiaries can vary according to the settlor's estate planning objectives, and the settlor may be a beneficiary but not the primary one. Many foreign jurisdictions also permit appointment of a trust "protector" who, as the title indicates, oversees the operation of the trust to insure its objectives are being met and the law is followed. A protector does not manage the trust but can veto actions in some cases.

Under U.S. tax law, foreign asset protection trusts are tax-neutral and are usually treated the same as domestic trusts, meaning income from the trust is treated as the settlor's personal income and taxed accordingly. Because the settlor retains some degree of control over the transfer of his assets to the foreign trust, U.S. gift taxes can usually be avoided. (But that degree of control can make the settlor vulnerable to court orders requiring him to exercise that control, thus defeating the asset protection he intended to gain.) Estate taxes are imposed on the value of trust assets for the settlor's estate, but all existing exemptions, such as those for marital assets, can be used. Asset protection trusts are not subject to the 35-percent U.S. excise tax imposed on transfers of property to a "foreign person."

As you will see in our discussion of partnerships in the next chapter, one device for a settlor to retain control of assets is to form a limited partnership and make the foreign asset protection trust a limited partner. This allows a general managing partner/settlor to retain control over all assets he transfers to the asset protection trust/limited partner abroad at the same time trust assets are theoretically protected from creditors or other legal attacks.

Some American court decisions recently have reduced the scope of asset protection of a limited partner, in cases holding that under certain circumstances assets can be attached by a judgment creditor, even though the people selling these programs often insist that the limited partnership is unassailable.

The greatest worry about a foreign asset protection trust often is the distance between you, your assets, and the people who manage them. (While your assets do not have to be transferred physically to the foreign country in which the trust exists, some circumstances may dictate such a precautionary transfer. Without such a transfer, a court could decide not to recognize the trust and take possession of the assets.)

If you are considering a foreign asset protection trust you should find out whether the foreign jurisdiction's laws are favorable, clear, and truly do offer the protection you seek. Examine the economic and political stability of the country, the reputation of its judicial system, local tax laws, the business climate, language barriers, and available communication and financial facilities. Unfortunately, there are very few U.S. experts in this field of asset protection law.

Several offshore financial centers have developed legislation hospitable to foreign-owned asset protection trusts, among them the Caribbean-area nations of the Cayman Islands, the Bahamas, Belize, St. Kitts-Nevis, the Turks and Caicos Islands, and the Cook Islands near New Zealand, as well as Cyprus and Gibraltar in the Mediterranean.

FAIR-WEATHER FINANCIAL PLANNING

An important consideration about foreign asset protection trusts—this arrangement will only work if it is planned and created at a time of financial calm, not in a personal crisis. If the foreign trust is set up when you are about to be (or have been) sued or are forced into bankruptcy, the act of transferring your assets to a foreign trust is likely to run afoul of strict fraudulent conveyance laws in the United States that protect creditors. These laws allow a court to declare a trust or any device used to conceal or remove assets from creditors as illegal and therefore void. If your assets are still within the court's jurisdiction, your having conveyed title to a foreign trustee is not likely to protect them from domestic attachment in such a case. If the assets actually are in the foreign jurisdiction, as in a bank account, the creditor will have more difficulty in reaching them before you can act to protect them.

OFFSHORE CORPORATIONS

Yet another legal device advocated by some as the perfect repository for asset protection is the creation of a corporation in a foreign nation ("offshore corporation"), which you as the instigator will control through various indirect means. The theory is that your corporate ownership will be concealed from the U.S. or other governments, allowing you financial privacy. The offshore corporation can hold legal title to foreign mutual funds or other valuable assets outside the United States, thus sheltering income and profits from American taxes. Business can be conducted through a designated nominee, thus shielding your secret participation from the prying eyes of creditors or the U.S. government.

In theory this sounds grand, but there are many practical problems associated with an offshore corporation.

First of all, just as required in establishing any domestic U.S. corporation, the legal formalities have to be strictly adhered to when you incorporate abroad, and the cost of setting up the company can be considerable. You will need foreign local legal counsel that knows the law and understands your asset protection objectives. Corporations anywhere are rule-bound creatures requiring separate books and records, meetings, minutes, and corporate authorizing resolutions that make it less flexible than many other arrangements.

Then there are the problems presented by U.S. tax law and court decisions upholding those laws. There is a U.S. tax on unrealized gains and income and capital gains taxes on transfers to foreign corporations. If the offshore company can be characterized as a "foreign personal holding company" the U.S. shareholder's portion of undistributed earnings will be taxed currently to him as ordinary income. The same IRS rule applies if the offshore entity qualifies as a "controlled foreign corporation," but additional taxes are imposed on gain derived from the sale of corporate assets. There is an established series of U.S. cases in which the courts have looked behind the offshore corporate veil and attributed "constructive ownership" to the U.S. taxpayer as an individual. Similar actual control findings have been based on a "chain of entities" linking the taxpayer to the corporation. The courts will look to who has substantive control as opposed to paper nominees who exercise nominal control. In addition, there are various specific IRS reporting requirements when an offshore corporation is created and when you serve as an officer, director, or 10 percent or greater shareholder in a foreign personal holding company or offshore corporation of any kind. The U.S. Supreme Court has even ruled that a U.S. taxpayer can be held guilty of "falsifying a federal income tax return" by maintaining he did not have certain foreign holdings and that Fourth Amendment guarantees regarding searches and seizures do not apply to documents located abroad pertaining to a U.S. taxpayer's ownership of foreign interests. And any unreported foreign corporation ownership is automatically a felony if it is discovered. When U.S. courts have concluded that offshore corporations are being used to conceal assets or avoid taxes, they have levied additional penalties and interest and often imposed criminal convictions.

A properly used foreign corporation can be part of an overall asset protection plan, but please don't rely on forming a quick corporation with bearer shares as a means of protecting your assets. Such shortcuts are only a pathway to disaster.

A RELIABLE SOURCE OF HELP

One of the best sources of help in setting up offshore trusts and corporations is an American certified accountant who has a large practice in Panama. Marc Harris holds a master's degree in business administration from Columbia University in New York and completed the Certified Public Accountancy Examination at the age of 18. He is believed to be the youngest person in the United States to pass the examination.

He opened his Panamanian firm in 1985, after being a consultant with the accounting firm of Ernst & Whinney. His services are highly recommended because he is able to create and administer off-shore corporations and trusts with complete compliance with U.S. laws. Often an American client uses a tax-haven-based advisor who knows the local laws but is not familiar with American tax law requirements and technicalities, and the client eventually gets into trouble, so Marc Harris has a unique ability to bridge the two worlds for his clients. Although based in Panama, he can create and administer corporations and trusts that are registered in all of the popular tax havens. His organization now has a staff of over 50 people. For more information, please write to The Harris Organization, Attn: Traditional Client Services, Estafeta El Dorado, Apartado Postal 6-1097, Panama 6, Panama.

Larry Abraham, in his newsletter *Insider Report*, said, "Over the years I have met and investigated numerous professionals . . . but the person and firm I have personally chosen to work with on these matters is Marc M. Harris of Panama.

"His firm is my first choice for anyone considering or preparing to move either assets or themselves into an off-shore posture. Marc Harris' offices in Panama City are well staffed, his people are efficient and professional, and, most importantly, he has a 'hands on' approach to everything that comes in the door."

By "hands on," Larry means that Harris and his staff actually do the work themselves and take full responsibility for it, instead of just giving advice.

CHAPTER 8

Using Tax Havens in Asset Protection

Many times people place corporations and trusts in tax havens. Depending upon the value and nature of the assets to be protected, this can be well worth the extra cost. The idea is that once a claimant has won his suit in the United States, he would then have to begin a new suit in the foreign country or countries in order to collect on the assets, in addition to whatever built-in protection there is through using such devices as foreign limited partnerships. And in the case of government forfeitures, the assets are well out of reach. Obviously if the foreign partnership owns U.S. real estate, not much has been accomplished, because it is too easy to attach the real estate itself and proceed in a U.S. court, ignoring the foreign judicial system. But if a family limited partnership registered in Guernsey has bank accounts in Luxembourg, an expensive nightmare has been created for the creditor, who may find it not worth proceeding, or who may be interested in negotiating a much lower settlement just to get something. For a fully detailed report on the various tax haven countries and the legal structures available in each, the best reference is *The Tax Haven Report* published by Scope International, Ltd., Box AS125, Forestside House, Forestside, Rowlands Castle, Hants, PO9 6EE, Great Britain. They will send a free catalog on request.

Another source of information is Eden Press, which publishes a series of special reports on different havens and techniques by which Americans can use them. You can obtain their catalog free by writing to them at P.O. Box 8410, Fountain Valley, CA 92728.

If you want to gain a good understanding of how the government views tax havens, University Microfilms International, through its Books On Demand program, is now making available *Tax Havens and Their Uses by United States Taxpayers* by Richard Gordon. Frequently referred to as "The Gordon Report," this was a 1981 U.S. Treasury Department study prepared at the request of Congress. It gives considerable detail and examples of the uses of tax havens. It is available from University Microfilms for $67.30 softbound, or $73.30 hardbound. Anyone interested in tax havens who has not studied the work out of print for more than a decade will find much still useful information in it. Copies can be ordered through booksellers, or directly from University Microfilms International, 300 North Zeeb Road, Ann Arbor, MI 48106-1346. The UMI catalog number of the book is AU00435, and UMI accepts Visa or MasterCard. (The catalog number is important, as UMI has more than 100,000 titles.)

In using tax havens for asset protection, you are not necessarily using either their tax advantages or their secrecy provisions. You are simply using them as a tax-neutral place to base these entities, while still paying your taxes and being able to disclose the assets should you need to in a lawsuit. By using tax havens for this purpose without being concerned with using secrecy provisions in the laws of the haven country, you don't put yourself in the position of committing perjury, and you haven't created some flimsy plan that falls apart as soon as there is the inevitable leak in your secrecy shield.

For similar reasons you are using the haven for its tax neutrality, to avoid adding foreign taxes to your situation, not as a way to avoid U.S. taxes.

Of course, in some cases, with careful planning, it is possible to achieve U.S. tax savings as well.

9

Asset Protection Using Swiss Annuities

Growing the wealth is important, but so is protecting it from false claimants, and Switzerland excels at this. Almost anybody with wealth in the U.S. is at risk, as discussed in the early sections of this report. With everything that can happen to savings, it is nice to know that there is something, somewhere, that nobody can touch.

According to Swiss law, insurance policies—including annuity contracts—cannot be seized by creditors. They also cannot be included in a Swiss bankruptcy procedure. Even if an American court expressly orders the seizure of a Swiss annuity account or its inclusion in a bankruptcy estate, the account will not be seized by Swiss authorities, provided that it has been structured the right way.

There are two requirements: A U.S. resident who buys a life insurance policy from a Swiss insurance company must designate his or her spouse or descendants, or a third party (if done so irrevocably) as beneficiaries. Also, to avoid suspicion of making a fraudulent conveyance to avoid a specific judgment, under Swiss law, the person must have purchased the policy or designated the beneficiaries not less than six months before any bankruptcy decree or collection process.

The policyholder can also protect the policy by converting a designation of spouse or children into an irrevocable designation when he becomes aware of the fact that his creditors will seize his assets and that a court might compel him to repatriate the funds in the insurance policy. If he is subsequently ordered to revoke the designation of the beneficiary and to liquidate the policy, he will not be able to do so as the insurance company will not accept his instructions because of the irrevocable designation of the beneficiaries.

Article 81 of the Swiss insurance law provides that if a policyholder has made a revocable designation of spouse or children as beneficiaries, they automatically become policyholders and acquire all rights if the policyholder is declared bankrupt. In such a case the original policyholder therefore automatically loses control over the policy and also his right to demand the liquidation of the policy and the repatriation of funds. A court therefore cannot compel the policyholder to liquidate the policy or otherwise repatriate his funds. If the spouse or children notify the insurance company of the bankruptcy, the insurance company will note that in its records. Even if the original policyholder sends instructions because a court has ordered him to do so, the insurance company will ignore those instructions. It is important that the company be notified promptly of the bankruptcy, so that they do not inadvertently follow the original policyholder's instructions because they weren't told of the bankruptcy.

If the policyholder has designated his spouse or his children as beneficiaries of the insurance policy, the insurance policy is protected from his creditors regardless of whether the designation is revocable or irrevocable. The policyholder may therefore designate his spouse or children as beneficiaries on a revocable basis and revoke this designation before the policy expires if at such time there is no threat from any creditors.

These laws are part of fundamental Swiss law. They were not created to make Switzerland an asset protection haven. There is a current fad of various offshore islands passing special legislation allowing the creation of asset protection trusts for foreigners. Since they are not part of the fundamental legal structure of the country concerned, local legislators really don't care if they work or not. And since most of these trusts are simply used as a convenient legal title to assets that are left in the U.S., such as brokerage accounts, houses, or office buildings, it is very easy for an American court to simply call the trust a sham to defraud creditors and ignore its legal title—seizing the assets that are within the physical jurisdiction of the court.

Such flimsy structures, providing only a thin legal screen to the title to American property, are quite different from real assets being solely under the control of a rock-solid insurance company in a major industrialized country. A defendant trying to convince an American court that his local brokerage account is really owned by a trust represented by a brass-plate under a palm tree on a faraway island is not likely to be successful; more likely the court will simply seize the asset.

But with the Swiss annuity, the insurance policy is not being protected by the Swiss courts and government because of any special concern for the American investor, but because the principle of protection of insurance policies is a fundamental part of Swiss law—for the protection of the Swiss themselves. Insurance is for the family, not something to be taken by creditors or other claimants. No Swiss lawyer would even waste his time bringing such a case.

Swiss annuities minimize the risk posed by U.S. annuities. They are heavily regulated, unlike in the U.S., to avoid any potential funding problem. They denominate accounts in the strong Swiss franc, compared to the weakening dollar. And the annuity payout is guaranteed.

Swiss annuities are exempt from the famous 35-percent withholding tax imposed by Switzerland on bank account interest received by foreigners. Annuities do not have to be reported to Swiss or U.S. tax authorities.

A U.S. purchaser of an annuity is required to pay a 1-percent U.S. federal excise tax on the purchase of any policy from a foreign company. This is much like the sales tax rule that says that if a person shops in a different state with a lower sales tax than his home state, when he gets home he is required to mail a check to his home state's sales tax department for the difference in sales tax rates.

The U.S. federal excise tax form (IRS Form 720) does not ask for details of the policy bought or who it was bought from—it merely asks for a calculation of 1-percent tax of any foreign policies purchased. This is a one-time tax at the time of purchase; it is not an ongoing tax. It is the responsibility of the U.S. taxpayer to report the Swiss annuity or other foreign insurance policy. *Swiss insurance companies do not report anything to any government agency, Swiss or American—not the initial purchase of the policy, nor the payments into it, nor interest and dividends earned.*

SPECIAL ADVANTAGES OF SWISS ANNUITIES

Swiss annuities bring together the benefits of Swiss bank accounts and Swiss deferred annuities without the drawbacks—presenting the best Swiss investment advantages for investors. The following is a list of the major advantages:

- *They pay competitive dividends and interest.*

- *No foreign reporting requirements.* A Swiss franc annuity is not a "foreign bank account," subject to the reporting requirements on the IRS Form 1040 or the special U.S. Treasury form for reporting foreign accounts. Transfers of funds by check or wire are not reportable under U.S. law by individuals—the reporting requirements apply *only* to cash and "cash equivalents"—such as money orders, cashier's checks, and travelers' checks.

- *No forced repatriation of funds.* If America were to eventually institute exchange controls, the government might require that most overseas investments be repatriated to America. This has been a common requirement by most governments that have imposed exchange controls. Insurance policies, however, would likely escape any forced repatriation under future exchange controls, because they are a pending contract between the investor and the insurance company. Swiss bank accounts would probably not escape such controls. (To the bureaucrats writing such regulations, an insurance policy is a commodity already bought, rather than an investment.)

- *Instant liquidity.* With most Swiss annuities, described later, an investor can liquidate up to 100 percent of the account without penalty (except for a SFr500 charge during the first year.).

- *Swiss safety.* Switzerland has the world's strongest insurance industry, with no failures in 130 years.

- *No Swiss tax.* If an investor accumulates Swiss francs through standard investments, he will be subject to the 35-percent withholding tax on interest or dividends earned in Switzerland. Swiss franc annuities are free of this tax. In the U.S., insurance proceeds are not taxed. And earnings on annuities during the deferral period are not taxable until income is paid or when they are liquidated.

- *Convenience.* Sending deposits to Switzerland is no more difficult than mailing an insurance premium in the United States. A personal check in U.S. dollars is written and sent overseas. Funds can also be transferred by bank wire.

- *Qualified for U.S. pension plans.* Swiss annuities can be placed in U.S. tax-sheltered pension plans, such as IRA, Keogh, or corporate plans, or such a plan can be rolled over into a Swiss annuity. (To put a Swiss annuity in a U.S. pension plan, all that is required is a U.S. trustee, such as a bank or other institution, and that the annuity contract be held in the United States by that trustee. Many banks offer "self-directed" pension plans for a very

small annual administration fee, and these plans can easily be used for this purpose.)

*   *No load fees.* Investment in Swiss annuities is on a "no
    load" basis, front-end or back-end. The investments can
    be canceled at any time, without a loss of principal, and
    with all principal, interest, and dividends payable if can-
    celed after one year. (If the investment is canceled in the
    first year, there is a small penalty of about 500 Swiss
    francs, plus loss of interest.)

Although called annuities, Swiss annuities act more like a savings account than a deferred annuity. But they are operated under
an insurance company's umbrella, so that they conform to the tax
man's definition of an annuity (in most countries, including the
United States) and, as such, compound tax-free until they are liquidated or converted into an income annuity later on.

Swiss annuity accounts earn approximately the same return as
long-term government bonds in the same currency the account is
denominated in (European Community bonds in the case of the
European Community Union or ECU), less a half-percent management fee.

Interest and dividend income are guaranteed by a Swiss insurance company. Swiss government regulations protect investors
against either underperformance or overcharging.

Swiss annuities offer instant liquidity, a rarity in annuities. All
capital, plus all accumulated interest and dividends, can be freely
accessible after the first year. During the first year 100 percent of the
principal is freely accessible, less a SFr 500 fee and loss of the interest. So if all funds are needed quickly, either for an emergency or for
another investment, there is no "lock-in" period.

Upon maturity of the account, the investor can choose
between taking a lump sum payout (paying capital gains tax on
accumulated earnings only), rolling the funds into an income annuity (paying capital gains taxes only as future income payments are
received, and then only on the portion representing accumulated
earnings), or extending the scheduled term by giving notice in

advance of the originally scheduled date (and continuing to defer tax on accumulated earnings).

Annuity Redemption Possibilities

Once you plan to redeem your investment or begin receiving an income, you have the following options:

1) You annuitize in full and receive a regular annual income for as long as you live.

2) You annuitize only a portion to provide for the life income you require at the time, and the remaining assets continue to accumulate earnings.

3) You liquidate in full, giving instructions on where to send the proceeds.

4) You liquidate only a portion, leaving the remaining assets to continue accumulating earnings.

Contact Information

The most practical way for North Americans to get information on Swiss annuities is to send a letter to a Swiss insurance broker specializing in foreign business. This is because very few transactions can be concluded directly by foreigners either with a Swiss insurance company or with regular Swiss insurance agents. They can handle the business legally, but they aren't used to it.

JML Swiss Investment Counsellors is an independent group of financial advisors. Since 1974 they have specialized in Swiss franc insurance, gold, and selected Swiss bank managed investments for overseas and European clients. At the time of publication the group was servicing more than 20,000 clients worldwide, with investments through JML of more than 1 billion Swiss francs. Their services are free of charge to you because they are paid by the renowned companies with which you invest your money. Their commissions and fees are standard, and all transactions are subject to strict regulation by the Swiss authorities.

All of their staff are fluent in English and understand the special concerns of the international investor. They know about all the many little details that are critical to you as a non-Swiss investor and have answers to your tax questions and other legalities. You can contact them using the following:

> JML Jurg M. Lattmann AG
> Swiss Investment Counsellors
> Baarerstrasse 53, Dept. 212
> CH-6304 Zug, Switzerland

When you contact JML, be sure to include, in addition to your name, address, and telephone number, your date of birth, marital status, citizenship, number of children and their ages, name of spouse, a clear definition of your financial objectives (possibly on what dollar amount you would like to invest), and whether the information is for a corporation or an individual, or both. A letter to get the current information is usually the most practical way to start.

A Swiss annuity for a portion of your assets can add a useful pillar to your overall protection plan, because it is something completely separate from your structure of family limited partnerships and living trusts and has its own independent set of protective rules. It also adds an extremely important diversification into a "hard money" asset.

CHAPTER 10

Protecting Precious Metals Investments

Gold is a traditional means of inflation protection. Some investors have been disappointed with the performance of gold in the past decade, but they are forgetting the primary purpose of gold as an inflation hedge. There has been very little inflation in the American economy in the past decade—so there has been nothing to be protected from. This does not mean that gold has been a bad investment. The proper comparison is not to other investment performance but to buying life insurance and not dying. The gold did exactly what it was supposed to do in the investor's portfolio—provided a store of value with inflation protection.

Gold is the most effective protection of purchasing power. This is illustrated by comparing its value today with its value in biblical times. From the Old Testament we learn that during the reign of King Nebuchadnezzar, an ounce of gold bought 350 loaves of bread. An ounce of gold today will still buy about 350 loaves of bread.

An investor who is paying attention to the current price of gold is missing the point completely.

Speculators have often lost badly with gold, but that is true of any speculation and is not because of some inherent characteristic of gold. This speculation is very different from the proper use of gold in an investment portfolio as a way of achieving balance, diversification, and inflation insurance.

Putting an entire savings program into diversified paper investments without a gold diversification is not a truly balanced plan. The security of the Swiss franc is one step toward that diversification because of the Swiss franc's strong gold backing and its traditional strength as a currency. But it is only a step. The next step is to diversify some of the portfolio into a pure gold investment.

Every paper currency buys less than it did at the turn of the century, but gold buys almost two times more. That is true inflation insurance and has nothing to do with overnight speculations on a belief in short-term price trends. There is nothing wrong with speculation, but it should not be confused with balancing the portfolio. In fact, a small percentage of any diversified portfolio is devoted to speculation.

Paper money inevitably declines in value and purchasing power. In an era when most governments have legally freed themselves from any requirement to act responsibly or tie their paper to real assets, this makes it particularly important for the investor to create his own "reserve fund," since the government's paper money no longer is required to have one.

For thousands of years, gold has been man's premier store of value, more trusted worldwide by individuals than any paper investment or paper currency. Gold cannot be inflated by printing more of it. It cannot be devalued by government decree. And, unlike paper currency or many other kinds of investments (such as stocks and bonds), gold is an asset that does not depend upon anybody's promise to repay.

Although gold has been mined for more than 6,000 years, only about 110,000 metric tons have ever been produced. If you could bring it all together, that is just enough to make a cube measuring only 18 meters (approximately 55 feet) along each side. Gold is one of the scarcest, and so most sought-after, metals on earth.

Gold cannot be fabricated by man. Nature limits its supply. The amount of new gold mined each year totals less than 2,000 metric tons—an amount that could fit comfortably into the living room of a small modern house.

Throughout recorded history, gold has held its value against inflation. Experts say, for example, that the same quantity of gold is needed to buy a loaf of bread today as in 16th-century England. This is why so many investors worldwide see it as the "ultimate asset"—an important and secure part of their investment portfolios.

Gold has an international value that tends to respond to the changes in value of national currencies. Time and again, gold has proved a successful hedge against the devaluation of an investor's national currency.

Gold is one of the few investments that has survived—and even thrived—during times of economic uncertainty. Gold is man's classic hedge against almost any monetary crisis, moving independently of paper investments.

For example, in the slump following the Wall Street crash, from September 1929 to April 1932, the Dow Jones Industrial Index slid from 382 to 56—a drop in value of 85 percent—and some 4,000 U.S. banks closed their doors. Meanwhile, the price of gold actually went up.

Gold also increased in value during the events following "Black Monday," October 19, 1987, when the Morgan Stanley index of world shares fell 19 percent over 10 days. And during the minicrashes that have afflicted the stock markets since then, gold has held its value and ignored the travails of share investment.

Gold is essentially a long-term investment with daily movements in price, and there is no tactic to ensure that you make your purchase at the best possible time.

One of the best ways to build up a keenly priced gold portfolio is to purchase relatively small amounts, on a regular basis, over an extended period. This is called "cost averaging." This will ensure that your total investment will have been acquired at the average gold price during the period of your investment program.

MOCATTA GOLD DELIVERY ORDERS

In recent years the purchase of gold bullion and coin "delivery orders" has become a popular form of ownership that avoids the inconvenience or safety concerns that arise with personal possession and storage. These orders are also available for silver and platinum.

A delivery order is a title document evidencing ownership of a specific serial number-identified bar of gold or silver bullion, or of specific gold, silver, or platinum coins packaged in a sealed numbered container unit. At the owner's option, the bullion or coins may be stored either in Zurich, Switzerland, or in Wilmington, Delaware. The depository chosen verifies the deposit by countersigning the delivery order.

Delivery orders are nonnegotiable, transferrable certificates that specifically identify the metals assigned to the order's owner and their physical location. The owner of the order can sell, assign, or collateralize it but is protected against loss or theft because of nonnegotiability. The metals identified are fully insured by Lloyds of London.

The delivery orders are issued by the Mocatta Metals Group, a worldwide trading consortium founded in 1671 specializing in precious metals with offices in New York, London, and Hong Kong.

The group's London affiliate, Mocatta and Goldsmid, is one of the five firms that officially participates in the twice-daily London gold price fixing, and M&G also chairs the daily silver price fixing.

Delivery orders from Mocatta for gold bullion are available in sizes of one kilobar (32.15 ounces), 100 and 400 ounce bars, and in gold coins including the Canadian Maple Leaf, American Eagle, Mexican 50 peso, and Austro-Hungarian 100 corona, available in quantities of 10. Silver and platinum coins are also available.

Buying a Mocatta delivery order means the purchaser owns specific metal identified on the order, which may be inspected at the storage place in Switzerland or Delaware. These metals may be removed by the owner or ordered to be shipped to any destination by endorsing and surrendering the delivery order.

Charges for delivery orders include a $100 issuance charge plus one year's storage charge, one half of one percent of the total value of the metal purchased, exclusive of the broker's sales commission. Usually there is no sales tax imposed.

The Mocatta delivery orders provide an easy method and a high degree of safety, liquidity, and privacy for your precious metals investing. MDOs offer transfer of ownership features that enable the owner to sell, assign, or collateralize the metal easily, yet provide the protection of nonnegotiability, since a lost document can be replaced, unlike a bearer security. Since the order is nonnegotiable, it does not have to be reported if it is taken in or out of the United States. There is no reporting of the purchase to the IRS. An MDO can be issued in the name of a family limited partnership or offshore trust, or assigned to one of them as a means of transferring ownership of the metal when the asset protection entity is created.

If you want more information about these orders, it may be obtained by contacting International Financial Consultants, Inc., Suite 400A, 1700 Rockville Pike, Rockville, MD 20852.

The Mocatta orders are also available in silver and platinum.

A SPECIAL PLAN—SWISSGOLD

"SwissGold" is the name used to describe a modern method allowing an individual to invest in gold with ease and assurance. It is a system based squarely on the protective, anti-inflation insurance aspects of gold, with none of the risks associated with gold contract futures or coin collecting gimmicks. And SwissGold is more efficient and economical than buying gold coins for their bullion content value through dealers.

SwissGold is a special investment account created by the respected UeberseeBank of Zurich, a medium-sized Swiss bank specializing in sound investment management. The bank does not engage in general commercial banking or lending to corporations or foreign governments, so it has no exposure to the risks inherent in such loans—and no conflicts of interest in managing investors' money for maximum results.

Founded in 1965, the bank now serves more than 12,000 clients, managing funds of almost US $3 billion. It is a wholly owned subsidiary of American International Group, Inc., one of the largest insurance holding companies. AIG has assets exceeding US $45 billion and capital of US $8.3 billion. It employs 33,000 people in more than 130 countries.

SwissGold is based on cost-averaging, rather than trying to out-guess the market. It is designed for simple and systematic savings—for example, an investor might decide to put $250 per month into gold. That $250 is going into gold every month, regardless of what the market does. In the long run the gold acquisition cost will be less than the average market price in the same period. This is called cost-averaging. It requires no market expertise from the investor—just the dedication to make the same fixed investment each month, regardless of the market. (In fact, some investors make a point of *not* looking at the market price.)

A similar technique is used by stock market investors; the cost-averaging principle is the same regardless of what is being bought. A fixed dollar amount is invested every month, rather than a fixed unit such as one share or one ounce being bought.

UeberseeBank handles the SwissGold accounts, sending detailed statements on each purchase of gold made for the investor. By purchasing in this manner, investors benefit from the bank's ability to buy at wholesale prices normally available only to large purchasers. In turn, the investor pays no extra fee on small unit amounts, nor does he pay the regular spread charged when buying and selling gold. These savings can be as much as 3 percent because of the wholesale price, and another 8 percent by avoiding small order surcharges. When added to the 20 percent savings that is often typical with cost-averaging, the investor is able to build the gold portion of his portfolio in the most economical way.

Naturally, such accounts are treated with the same secrecy as any other Swiss bank account. Each investor's gold is held separately by the bank acting as trustee in a fiduciary relationship. This arrangement is legally significant, because it means the amount of gold in the SwissGold account is always the investor's property, not merely a gold denominated paper obligation of the bank. Thus solvency or credit standing of the bank cannot affect the investor's holdings, although a bank failure in Switzerland is almost unimaginable even with a commercial bank—and UeberseeBank does not even assume commercial risks.

Of course, the gold is insured as well as securely guarded, and the investor can choose to have it stored in Switzerland, the United States, or Canada.

SwissGold accounts can be tailored to an investor's needs, and flexibility is the key word. An investor can suspend gold purchases at any time without penalty, and account possibilities range from monthly purchases to large lump sum purchases, depending upon the individual investor's needs.

Should you have any concern about investing in gold through a Swiss bank like Uebersee, you should know that banking in Switzerland is a national source of not only income but great pride as well. Operating in a country less than half the size of the state of Maine, Swiss banks control more than $400 billion in assets, making Switzerland the third largest financial center in the world after London and New York.

For people with money to protect—whether a little or a lot—Switzerland is traditionally considered the world's safest repository. These days, the Swiss can give Americans many reasons to leave funds in Switzerland—SwissGold is one of them—but the promise of total secrecy in financial matters remains one of the greatest attractions of Swiss banks.

Swiss statutory civil law protects the customer and the customer's financial dealings as part of the individual's legal right to privacy. As Article 28 of the Swiss Civil Code, this law not only protects such information, but makes the person violating secrecy liable to pay damages to the customer. In addition, the banking law makes it a criminal offense for a bank or any of its employees to divulge information about a customer, punishable by fine or imprisonment.

Information on SwissGold accounts may be obtained from:

JML Jurg M. Lattmann AG
Swiss Investment Counsellors
Baarerstrasse 53, Dept. 212
CH-6304 Zug, Switzerland

The firm specializes in assisting American and English investors, and everybody speaks your language.

CHAPTER

11

Privacy Tactics That Can Give You an Advantage

There are a number of little things that can help you to protect your privacy—and make your assets just a bit less visible. This chapter highlights several little-known options that you may find useful.

USE A STAND-ALONE TELEPHONE CALLING CARD

Intended for travelers who use calling cards frequently, there is a discount telephone calling card that has a flat rate of 17.5 cents per minute for interstate calls, anytime, anywhere in the United States including Puerto Rico, Hawaii, Alaska, and the U.S. Virgin Islands. There are no surcharges, no monthly fees, no minimum monthly billings, and *international calling is also available*.

The calling card is free and is a stand-alone card, meaning that a person using the card does not have to switch long distance services.

It saves up to 68 percent over the leading competitors, including pre-paid phone cards (most of which are around 40 cents per minute).

But it is the "stand-alone" part that makes it worth mention-ing here. Because the card can be applied for without having to sub-scribe to a new long distance service, one can use the card for things like calling overseas banks and pay the separate calling card bill from a different bank account or by money order. The record of calls made won't be showing up on your home or office phone bill, so there's no easy-to-follow trail of calls to an offshore bank or money manager. And since the separate calling card bill can be paid by money order, it doesn't create a credit card charge record, which is one of the problems in recharging prepaid phone cards. (And you don't get an embarrassing "out of time" recording and cut-off, which can easily happen on a prepaid card when a $10 card is being used for an expensive overseas call.)

For an application form, send a stamped, addressed reply enve-lope to:

> Center for Business Information
> Attn: Phone Card Applications
> 816 Elm Street, Suite 187
> Manchester, NH 03101-2101

HOW TO KEEP THE IRS—AND OTHER SNOOPS—
OUT OF YOUR SAFE DEPOSIT BOX

A safe deposit box is a veritable necessity for keeping things like offshore bank books, precious metals certificates, bearer secu-rities, cash, coins, and so on. Yet a safe deposit box can create its own problems.

One obvious problem is that upon death of the box holder, the bank is required to deny access to the box until a properly appoint-ed executor and an IRS agent open the box. The IRS will presume that all assets are the property of the deceased, so that if you are holding assets that you have given in trust to your children, they will become part of the taxable estate—or worse, they may be applied to some debt of the estate. Unreported foreign accounts could even be seized as being part of a crime. IRS agents tend to assume criminality, and you are no longer available to provide an alternative honest explanation.

But there are other safe deposit box problems that are at least as important as dealing with the box upon death. For example, if the box is in one name only, many banks will not honor a power of attorney to let somebody else have access to the box in an emergency, unless the power of attorney is signed in person at the bank. If you are in a foreign hospital and need to authorize your spouse to open the box, this could become a major problem. Even if the bank will accept a notarized power of attorney, there may be problems in arranging for a foreign notary to visit, then having the notary certificate authenticated by the U.S. Embassy or Consulate and sent to the bank.

The solution is to form a corporation to hold your principal safe deposit box. The corporation can change the names of the people authorized to access the box simply by furnishing the bank with an updated resolution form. And a box belonging to a corporation is not frozen by a bank because of the death of a person, even if that person is the sole individual then having access to the box.

For this to be done properly, we recommend that the corporation be used only to hold the safe deposit box. This provides the maximum privacy because the corporation has no activities to cause it to be audited or investigated. Under federal law, even an inactive corporation must file a tax return, but it can file a corporate return each year showing no income without having to pay an accountant to do it. (Usually after three years of zero-income returns, the IRS sends out a form letter saying there is no need to file further returns unless the corporation begins to have income.)

The other obligation that must be met is to ensure that the corporation is in good standing so that you don't have a crisis in which the corporation no longer exists because the annual reports were not filed. Delaware is the best state for this, because an inactive corporation only needs to file a simple annual return and pay an annual fee to the state (and an annual fee to its Delaware-registered agent).

Privacy can be maintained by having the registered agent file the annual return with the state, signing it as "incorporator," which keeps the list of officers off the state records. Most large corporation services will not provide annual report filing services, but the one mentioned below will do so. To be entirely safe, one can even leave the registered agent with funds to prepay the state fees each year, thus ensuring that there is no accidental termination of the corporation because of a late payment.

Since the holding of a safe deposit box is not deemed to be conducting business by any state, the Delaware corporation is not required to qualify to do business in the state in which the box is held, thus improving privacy and keeping the existence of the corporation out of the public records in your own state.

For information on a service that can form a corporation for you in Delaware (or in any state), write to the following address:

INC PLAN USA
Attn: Incorporation Information Package
802 West Street
Wilmington, DE 19801

Keeping the IRS away is not the only reason to have a corporation hold your safe deposit box. It also keeps a personal creditor from being able to have the box frozen by a court for an inspection of the contents, which can easily happen during a lawsuit or other claim against you.

PRIVACY AND DATA ENCRYPTION

Your business affairs are your personal matter. Encryption is an electronic procedure that digitally encodes (converts into unintelligible gibberish) and decodes (converts back to readable language).

Today any reasonably powerful desktop computer can encrypt and decrypt messages that the most powerful supercomputers in the world, working together, could not decrypt. Programs to do this are very inexpensive and already available to anyone.

Most encryption programs take advantage of a mathematically sophisticated encryption technology that requires two different keys, both of which are necessary to decrypt the message. The sender needs only one to send a message. The receiver decodes the message with the second key—which never needs to leave his computer, where it can be protected by passwords. Although the mathematics are daunting, the program makes the process simple and straightforward.

Examples of everyday uses are a writer who sends chapters of his new book to his publisher, collaborators on an invention working at a distance and needing to keep others from claim-jumping a discovery, a consumer paying bills or ordering from mail-order catalogs by sending encrypted credit card numbers over the telephone, an accountant who scrambles backup tapes so that clients needn't worry about lost confidentiality if the tapes are lost or stolen, and attorneys communicating with clients and other attorneys via encrypted documents.

At the same time, the costs of international communications and transportation have declined to the point where even the average individual can afford to internationalize. And countries around the world are competing for that business. You can take advantage of what these countries have to offer to safeguard your freedom and privacy using exactly the same techniques as giant multinational companies.

Encrypted messages can move without interference across international borders by telephone, by radio, or by courier. A "message" means anything that can be digitized—a sequence of words, music, a digitized picture, a forbidden magazine or book, and so on.

Privacy of electronic communications leads to an ability to do business from anywhere in the world, with anybody in the world.

It is technically feasible to use these techniques to create a totally secret banking system, with account owners' identities being unknown even to the bank. Credits could be transferred between accounts from anywhere in the world through encrypted communications. In a world where governments are increasingly subscribing to treaties limiting banking secrecy and requiring identification of depositors, it is unlikely that this technical possibility will actually occur in the near future. But unlikely is not impossible, and the time may come when some government permits such a service, or when entrepreneurs sneak it in the back door by calling it a barter exchange instead of a bank. Since everything is electronic, such a service could even be operated from a ship, an orbiting space station, or the moon. It is only 30 years since the first moon landing—who knows what the next 30 years might bring. The data haven may eventually supplement the tax haven.

Meanwhile, data encryption is available to everybody for whatever use they wish to make of it. A package offering basic information on encryption, including copies of several different computer programs on 3.5" diskette for IBM-compatible computers, is called "The Encryption Collection" and is available for $50 from the following supplier:

> Scope International, Ltd.
> Forestside House, Box AS125
> Forestside, Rowlands Castle, Hants, PO9 6EE
> Great Britain

With the U.S. government making proposals to outlaw the sale of encryption programs, this is something you might want to buy now and put away even if you have no immediate use for it. Several European countries have already banned the use of encryption by their citizens.

Don't Do Illegally What You Can Do Legally

One of the greatest problems of asset protection planning is the naive fool who breaks laws without thinking through the consequences.

So many people think that using secrecy instead of a carefully made plan is the solution to their problem. There is no such thing as a "secret" bank account for an American, because it is a felony to fail to immediately notify the government of the existence of the account. The penalties for such secrecy are far worse than any possible tax offense—and recently the penalties have been increased so severely that no American should even contemplate such a violation. One bribed bank clerk (perhaps for a mere $100) in a so-called secrecy jurisdiction could put the client in prison for 10 to 15 years under new mandatory minimum sentencing laws.

There are so many legitimate ways that a U.S. citizen can have asset protection without running afoul of these draconian laws, as this book has shown you, that nobody needs to do illegally what one can do legally.

The most dangerous fools—to themselves as well as to everyone they deal with—are those individuals who fail to understand the serious implications of their actions. They deal with lawyers, accountants, and/or bankers as if there was nothing legally wrong with their actions and then seem startled when the family accountant or banker facing many years in prison testifies against them because he was dragged into something he had no intention of being a part of. Or worse, they wind up blurting out their incriminating intentions to a lawyer or accountant who immediately notifies the authorities, frequently setting a trap for them. (Remember, lawyer-client confidentiality does not apply to stating an intention to commit a crime, and the lawyer is legally obligated to report it.) Many U.S. professionals today (perhaps fearing a possible set-up by authorities) venture on the side of caution and immediately report such approaches. This is no secret; it has been recorded in many, many court cases, but the naive clients continue to get convicted.

Most of these people would never consider committing a bank robbery, and if they were to plan such a crime they would choose their partners with extreme care and full awareness of the consequences by all parties concerned. Yet they think nothing of committing financial crimes with far more serious penalties and cavalierly involving others as if it were a big joke and nothing to be seriously concerned about. This couldn't be further from the truth; the penalties for most bank secrecy and money laundering crimes (money laundering includes moving unreported cash, even if you are the legal owner) are several times the penalty for armed bank robbery.

ABOUT THE AUTHOR

Adam Starchild is the author of more than a dozen books and hundreds of magazine articles, primarily on business and finance. His articles have appeared in a wide range of publications around the world, including *Business Credit*, *Euromoney*, *Finance*, *The Financial Planner*, *International Living*, *Offshore Financial Review*, *Reason*, *Tax Planning International*, *Trusts & Estates*, and many more.